T0268934

Dr. Rice in the House

Edited by Amy Scholder

Seven Stories Press
New York I Toronto I London I Melbourne

A Seven Stories Press First Edition

"The Ode to Condoleezza Rice" is an excerpt from Coco Fusco's performance script, *A Room of One's Own: Women and Power in the New America*. The full script is published in *The Drama Review*, 51, 4 (T196) Winter 2007.

Amiri Baraka's "Somebody Blew up America" first appeared on www.amiribaraka.com.

Seven Stories Press
140 Watts Street
New York, NY 10013
www.sevenstories.com

In Canada: Publishers Group Canada, 559 College Street, Suite 402, Toronto, ON M6G 1A9

In the UK: Turnaround Publisher Services Ltd., Unit 3, Olympia Trading Estate, Coburg Road, Wood Green, London N22 6TZ

In Australia: Palgrave Macmillan, 627 Chapel Street, South Yarra, VIC 3141

College professors may order examination copies of Seven Stories Press titles for a free six-month trial period. To order, visit www.sevenstories.com/textbook or send a fax on school letterhead to (212) 226-1411.

Book and cover design by Rex Ray Studio

Library of Congress Cataloging-in-Publication Data

Dr. Rice in the house / edited by Amy Scholder. -- Seven Stories Press 1st ed.
    p. cm.
 Includes bibliographical references.
 ISBN 978-1-58322-761-9 (pbk.)
1. Rice, Condoleezza, 1954---Miscellanea. 2. Rice, Condoleezza, 1954---Influence--Miscel-
lanea. 3. Rice, Condoleezza, 1954--Political and social views--Miscellanea. 4. Stateswomen--
United States--Miscellanea. 5. Women cabinet officers--United States--Miscellanea. 6. African
American women--Miscellanea. 7. African Americans--Race identity--Miscellanea. 8. United
States--Politics and government--2001---Miscellanea. 9. United States--Race relations--Political
aspects--Miscellanea. I. Scholder, Amy. II. Title: Doctor Rice in the house.

E840.8.R48D7 2007
327.730092--dc22
[B]
                                    2007005175

Printed in Canada.

9 8 7 6 5 4 3 2 1

DR. RICE IN THE HOUSE

DR. RICE IN THE HOUSE
A Preface

Amy Scholder

When Condoleezza Rice was appointed national security advisor in George W. Bush's first term in 2000, she was part of the most diverse administration the US had ever seen. (She was among Colin Powell, Elaine Chao, Ann Veneman, Karen Hughes, Christine Todd Whitman, Gale Ann Norton, and others.) Democrats were shamed by the fact that one of the most reactionary presidents of the past hundred years could appear more racially and gender balanced in his cabinet appointments than his predecessors. The Republicans were shrewd. As they scored points with swing voters by seeming inclusive, they have implemented draconian policies that have chipped away at the gains made by the civil rights, women's and lesbian/gay movements for social justice and equality. The Patriot Act, the Gay Marriage Amendment, and the dismantling of affirmative action are only a few of the reactionary crusades they have taken on. And there has been no one more fitting—and willing—to front these cynical politics than Dr. Rice. Her corporate and academic credentials proved that before becoming a government official, she could work her way into the white world and take her place at the table. And according to her, she has no one to thank but herself.

As one of the world's most powerful public figures, Condoleezza Rice, it would seem, would be the subject of a steady stream of articles, essays, investigative reports, and books published about her contribution to world affairs. Instead, she has become the focal point of countless articles and radio and TV talk shows, centered not on her work as national security advisor and secretary of state, but on Rice as a public figure about whom we want to know more personally. Americans in particular want to feel intimate with "Condi." What does she have for breakfast? What is her exercise regime? How does she stay so slim? Who is she wearing? What do we make of her hair? (The answer to that question alone could take up volumes.) On Sunday, April 9, 2006, the *New York Times* ran a full-page, "human interest" story on Condoleezza Rice's passion for playing the piano (". . . in spite of being extremely busy, Rice regularly plays piano with string-playing lawyer friends . . ."). What else was Rice doing that week on behalf of the American public? And why is this the sort of reporting we see, even in the newspaper of record? When the coverage on Rice is not personal, it often puts her in the middle of the ongoing debates about race, class and gender in America. Being an African-American woman from Birmingham, Alabama has given her a credibility that liberals and conservatives alike find irresistible. And she actively perpetuates the myth that race and gender are no longer barriers to success.

Obviously Condoleezza Rice holds a special place in the national imagination. And the spectacle of "Condi" has served the administration well, diverting difficult and more essential questions that should be posed to her or to anyone in her position. When she served on the Chevron board of directors (and then had a tanker named in her honor), how did she live with the knowledge of the environmental and human costs of drilling in the Niger Delta? Does she really believe in the morality of torture and rendition? Has the mass destruction sponsored by US foreign policy since 9/11 brought any nation—including ours—closer to the ideals of democracy?

In this volume, there is thoughtful consideration of Condoleezza Rice by some of the most challenging and innovative writers, artists and scholars of our time—responses to Rice as a political force, as a cultural phenomenon and as a Black woman in a world dominated by white men. This is the first collection dedicated to Dr. Rice and her powerful influence. It also serves as an index of where the culture wars of the 1990s have ended up: it is revealing of our times to consider how a Black woman fronting right-wing forces is received and considered by the public and her peers.

When I began gathering contributions for this book, the Republicans had just been ushered into a second term, and mass media were yet to challenge the Bush administration and, in particular, the foreign policy carried out by the secretary of state. We may wonder what Rice thinks about voters' unwillingness in the mid-term elections to stay the course of the current administration's policies in Iraq and around the world, which she so skillfully fronts. One thing we know for sure is that we can't take anything she says or does at face value.

ODE TO CONDOLEEZZA

Coco Fusco

Madame Secretary, I send you greetings not only from me but also from all the soldiers under my command. We are all so very proud to support your leadership in our nation's foreign affairs. Knowing that today is your birthday, I thought it fitting to send you this videotaped message. It's a poem. I wrote it—well, actually I adapted it for you. I hope you like it.

Scene from performance of *A Room of One's Own:*
Women and Power in the New America

photo by Kambui Olujimi

ODE TO CONDOLEEZZA

When our country's cause provokes to arms,
How your sweet music every bosom warms!
When in our world tumultuous wars arise,
Music your soft, persuasive voice applies;
When our cabinet is pressed with cares,
You exalt them with enlivening airs.
Foreign leaders, all such skeptics–
are undone by your insightful rhetoric.
Envious radicals how they scorn,
Hapless liberals are left forlorn.
'Tis your quiet force that stops all terror,
Not those filibusters or Congressional errors.
Your music the fiercest chief can charm,
Islam's severest rage disarm.
Your melodies soften pain to ease,
And make despair and madness please.
Our joys below it can improve,
When sense you impart to government's moves.
All others to your grace aspire;
Your sounds lift soldiers' spirits higher,
And angels lean from heaven to hear.
Of other brave women may no pundit tell,
To Condoleezza greater power is given;
Bin Laden plunged us into hell,
She lifts our souls to heaven.

Happy Birthday, Madame Secretary!

IT'S NOT ABOUT THE HAIR

Jill Nelson

Condoleezza Rice is hard to fathom. She insists on placing herself and her life experience almost wholly outside the context of African-American life in the last half of the twentieth century. Rice would have us believe that the crucial and transformative events that touched the lives of all Americans, particularly those of us who came of age in the 1950s and 60s, were not relevant to her life. The movements that profoundly changed the lives of not only Black Americans, but all Americans, particularly the Civil Rights Movement, the Black Power Movement, the Women's Movement, and even the Anti-Vietnam War Movement, apparently skipped over Rice, with her taking no or little notice.

The core of the narrative of Rice's formative years is one absent the collective struggle born from the recognition of the collective oppression and disenfranchisement of African Americans and women. If Rice's life were a movie, the theme song would be Frank Sinatra singing, "My Way," and the screen would be awash with images of a determined Rice making it through adversity on a path composed of a strong family, intelligence, and sheer determination.

Rice posits her youth and her adult achievements in a way that is almost ahistorical, as if the context and content of the times she lived in had no effect upon her, positive or negative. This is a stunning departure both from what we know from the historical records about Negro life in America—particularly in Birmingham, Alabama, where Rice grew up, a town whose response to the mere prospect of integration was so violent that it was nicknamed "Bombingham"—in 1954, the year Rice was born. Her refusal to acknowledge the suffering and trauma of such race violence is more disturbing when one considers the fact that a childhood playmate of hers was killed in Birmingham's most heinous incident, the 1963 bombing of the Sixteenth Street Baptist Church. And Rice's assertions that she just sort of ignored racism and was therefore unaffected by it, another aspect of her "I did it my way with the help of a strong, educated, middle class family" is nearly unbelievable. If it is true it is not only deeply troubling, but downright frightening. Do we really want one of the closest advisors to a president who prides himself on being disengaged and out of touch to be equally so? Yet that appears to be exactly who we've got.

It's bizarre that as an African-American woman born in New York City in 1952, two years before Rice's birth in Birmingham, I apparently had and have gained more understanding of the profound (and important) impact the Civil Rights Movement had, not only on my life, but all Black lives and on most other American lives as well. Unlike Rice, I didn't go to church down the street from the church (Sixteenth Street Baptist Church) where Denise McNair, Cynthia Wesley, Carole Robertson and Addie Mae Collins were blown up by a racist's bomb in 1963, a few weeks after the historic march on Washington, but I was frightened, hurt, and outraged by this event, and the many others like it—the murders of civil rights activists Chaney, Schwerner, Goodman, and Viola Luizzo; the assassination of Medgar Evers, head of the NAACP in Mississippi; and on and on and on.

It's difficult to believe that at twelve and a thousand miles away—and there were no "Whites Only" or "Colored" signs in Manhattan, where I grew up—I understood what Rice apparently did not: that the violence in response to the Civil Rights Movement was not only ghastly and profoundly important but personal.

Not only to individuals, but to all Black people, all right thinking people, and to America. It signalled to all of us that resistance would be met with murder, even the murder of children, and that those who stood up could not even expect justice for the murder of their young, their loved ones, or their leaders.

I am not alone. Talk with any Black person who was over the age of six or seven in 1963 and it's a safe bet that they too were touched and transformed by these events and others like them over the decade. In my home, as in many, many others, the Southern Civil Rights Movement was a constant and usually complex topic of conversation. Dr. King's nonviolence versus Malcolm X's militancy. Activism in the courts, the streets or both. The positive and negative effects of Rap Brown's call for "Black Power." The Black Panther Party's simultaneous armed policing of the police and feeding school kids in their breakfast programs. John F. Kennedy, Lyndon Johnson, Fannie Lou Hamer, the riots or rebellion, the struggle for civil rights and social justice. These topics were like a talkative aunt who comes for a visit and never leaves or lets up.

It is unfathomable that while all this was going on Condoleezza Rice was marching to her own individualist drummer, essentially oblivious to the seismic shifts in American society that would change all of our lives. But that doesn't mean it's not possible. What's impossible to understand or believe is that as a grown woman she studiously perpetuates this obliviousness. As if the Civil Rights, Black Power, Women's Rights, and Anti-War Movements didn't change our world, reshape everything in ways that left none of us untouched, even if we, like those angry white men and so-called Christian homophobes, wish it weren't so. Recognize it or not, these events made it possible for there to be a Black female Secretary of State, even one who is anti-Black, postfeminist, culturally Eurocentric, and apparently can't find anyone to put a decent hairdo on her head.

Not unlike doctoring a resume to make one's achievements seem greater than they are, Condoleezza Rice has created an essentially fictitious narrative to gain entry into the club of right-wing Republican powerbrokers. This fiction is, in turn, not unlike George W. Bush's successful electoral projection of himself as a simple Texas good ol' boy, a fella the average American could sit down and have a beer with, instead of a privileged son of the Eastern elite.

Similarly, the portraits drawn of themselves by both Rice and Bush are tailored to appeal to specific constituencies, for specific reasons. In Rice's case, it seems that she realized early on that positioning herself as the "Only One"—Black, female, Republican true believer—would increase the educational, professional and economic opportunities from which most of the country, and the vast majority of people of color, are excluded. Her family's decision to move her from school to school in Birmingham so that she could adapt to various, probably unwelcoming, educational environments set her course. Escaping the rigidly segregated life of Alabama for Colorado and taking up early pursuits of training in ice skating and classical music (both avocations that actually require engagement and personal expression) were choices that certainly would have set her apart at the time, followed by the coup de grâce, choosing to pursue an area of studies concentrating on Russia. From the time she elected to become a Russian scholar, she became the "exceptional Negro" in any room she entered. In recent years, this same strategy has been used effectively by Clarence Thomas, Ward Connolly, Armstrong Williams, and others.

These similar narratives perpetuate the myth of the meritocracy, in which those who work hard rise to the top on the strength of the merits and receive their just deserts. It is a myth that necessarily exists outside all contexts: political, economic, social, historical, since the slightest brush with context inevitably reveals the myth as just that.

This is not to suggest that Rice isn't intelligent—although as Laura Flanders has pointed out, she wasn't sharp enough to see the fall of the Soviet Union coming—but, as a college dean I know used to say, quoting his grandma, "Education is a wonderful thing—if you're smart." Which speaks, I think, to the uses to which one puts their education, a department in which Condoleezza Rice's achievements—earning a Ph.D., becoming provost of

Stanford University, serving on the board of the oil giant Exxon, serving as a Sovietologist in the administration of Bush Sr. and as national security advisor and now secretary of state in the administration of Bush Jr.—fall short.

It's telling that the two most prominent Negros in the Bush administration, Colin Powell and Condoleezza Rice, both achieved individual prominence via routes that reject the collective action or consciousness of Black people. Powell chose the military, where obedience to authority is paramount (though his rise in the service was made possible by protests forcing integration in the 1940s) and Rice, who benefited similarly from the legacy of past activism, opted for a denial that civil rights laws, affirmative action, women's rights, or liberalism had anything to do with her success. Yet I am hard pressed to think of one important thing that Black Americans have achieved that did not either require or come as a result of a collective rejection of an oppressive authority. The other benefit to this me-only opportunism is that no debts are owed to those who have gone before or to the community at large. People such as Rice have no coattails, bring no opportunities for others, and are able to hold themselves aloof from accountability to their communities, the nation, or even those citizens of the world who suffer from their most dangerous decisions. They have no ties to the rest of us, have no need to listen to the public they serve, and speak for no one but themselves in the chambers of power.

People I know who know her say that Condoleezza Rice is a lovely person, and maybe she is, but just as I see no value in a president I wanna have a brewski with, it's irrelevant if Condoleezza is a nice person and can cook her ass off when she's off duty. She may not want to claim the personal impact of our collective Negro and American history, but no ingenious narrative will allow her to absent herself from her role in creating the volatile, grim world of this new millennium. What's ironic and telling is that Rice, who denies the impact of collective activism on her own personal life, is a crucial member of one of the most activist presidencies in history. Apparently it's only collective action in service of the oppressed and disenfranchised that she can't see, relate to, or be tainted by. The top-down activism of the Bush administration is about as beneficial as trickle-down economics.

When it comes to the Bush administration's destruction of democracy at home, contempt for nations abroad, and heaping economic rewards on allies, Rice has no such qualms. Quite the contrary, she places herself in the vanguard of the right-wing transformation being imposed on citizens of the United States and the world, although this activism is couched as policy, diplomacy, and her mandate as secretary of state.

Perhaps what profoundly grates on me about Condoleezza Rice is that she places herself outside the essential and varied notions of Black community that are critical parts of the narrative of Black women's lives, particularly our public lives. One may not be able to draw a straight line from Harriet Tubman to Oprah, but the connections in terms of history, experience, and commitment are, if not obvious, discernible.

Not so to Rice, who stands alone, insistently spinning a lonely narrative of individual hard work and triumph, a cover story that in this nation founded on genocide and slave labor has never been real. That she has risen to the top does not justify the service to which her energies and intellect have been applied. As suspicious as her past narrative of individual achievement absent collective struggle is, the chickens have truly come home to roost. Today, Condoleezza Rice stands exactly where she's worked to get, alone, the only Black woman to have contributed so mightily to making the world a far more terrible and terrifying place.

A WHITER SHADE OF BLACK
Reflections Concerning Condoleezza Rice and Her Curious Ilk

Gary Indiana

There is always someone who feels faulted and swindled who is willing. Willing is an essential function of the mind. You can find plenty of people willing their own destruction, and that of people around them. Manipulative calculation; willing. Related but not yet universally synonymous. Leaders and followers take the same suicidal path on different tracks. The victim can become the torturer without self-doubt or introspection. There is always one and most often many more than one who can refine the traumas recollected from days that lost their sting but never their utilitarian effectiveness in a land of guilt and charades of equality. Whole countries cling to ancient persecutions like cherished teddy bears stuffed with ball bearings to batter people into acquiescence with their own persecution of the people they've fashioned into enemies, to avoid moral atonement for the violence they unleash.

And there is always room for one of every otherwise despised creature on the lifeboat, sometimes even places for two or three. They will be used later on when the provisions run out to stem the shrinking supply of protein and fat.

The captain and his crew never need to define themselves, to fix a name on what they are. It's for us, or those of us who don't mind reducing our identity to something as shallow as skin and trivial as what kind of genitalia appeal to us and bogus as the righteousness of gender politics that don't apply, when we're offered that seat in the lifeboat, playing the beaten-down African American, the gay kid who suffered all the torments of hell in high school, the woman wronged by every man she ever met and held back in her ambitions despite her superior talents: it's all very useful for staking out that one place in the lifeboat.

The magazine has one black writer. Sometimes it goes so far as to publish two black writers within the same year. If something really black and terrible occurs, you may even find both of them in the same issue.

There was never such a thing as a gay writer until some enterprising homosexual decided that he would be the one homosexual to make it into the lifeboat, convincing the credulous (nearly everybody) that Proust and Gide and hundreds before him had indicated their sexual tastes so casually out of fear, and not because they had more important things to write about. Our avatar of the insistently gay decided to strike the pose of the serious writer, the highbrow *litterateur*, and he was good at it, albeit sanctimonious and unbearably mannered and really not terribly bright. Several years later a buffoon was sought out to make homosexuality something cute and harmless, a laugh riot for crowds who would give him an autopsy while he was still breathing if the wind shifted. Eventually both secured spaces on the lifeboat, the clown near the rudder and the *Petit Proust pour les decorateurs dans le Marais* near the helm, and the Captain let them on because, as long as they served the larger purpose, they could be considered two completely different things, almost.

What all the exceptionally determined anomalies offered the other survivors besides entertainment was a genuine facility for advancing the world's appetite for the fraudulent, the nauseatingly sincere, and the globalizing structure's allergy to anything authentic, or even slightly truthful. They invented, or perhaps rediscovered, a phenomenon associated with historical amnesia and a hysterical fear of facts. Blanketing the world with the pretense that something is new because a new person, for whom the past is an inky void, has brought a feeble imitation of something better but forgotten to the marketplace, has defined the culture of the past twenty years. It's important for some cartoon of culture to make it on board, crafting little items to fructify various cargo cults the survivors may encounter on their seemingly uncharted route. To make the lifeboats before the whole shithouse sinks requires demonstrating real conviction that "smart for the stupid" not only works better but is vastly preferable to "smart for the smart" or "do unto others as you would have them do unto you."

Every man for himself, Captain Nemo, and god against all, and now we've made a lot of these people's brains softer than eiderdown so that we can get them to eat their dead grandmothers before they'd dare mutiny for a decent wage or join a union. We can set them debating until they drown in steerage whether some troglodyte we painted brown is a scapegoat for Fu Manchu or hated for being a woman; give the pansies enough money and they suddenly think they're better than the niggers, get the dykes back into femme lipstick and butch whiffle cuts like the 1950s and crazy as it sounds, people only see what we show them and think what we tell them to. If you want them to fall into line with the biggest lies ever told, cut to a little girl who fell down a well and cover that nail-biting rescue mission 24/7 until some more of their rights are safely quashed by some act of Congress they never heard of. Get them revved to drink the Kool-Aid, get them used to the wound culture. No community without a catastrophe going on. Hide the real wounds behind the curtain so the Wizard of Shit can promise them everything and give them nothing.

Language is only useful to power when it's used not to mean anything. Condoleezza Rice is, like everyone in the Bush Cabal, adept at saying nothing that sounds like something. They can telegraph in three or four words the lie of the day and this economy of verbalization, the breathtaking clarity of the mantras minted to turn reality inside out, takes theatrical illusion beyond farce into an aggressive insistence on suspension of disbelief—what we call in the theater, "demonic abandon."

The left had a language, a lot of it vehement and unreasonable even when there was logic behind it. When you go too far abusing language your enemy can turn the same words and the concepts they represent (without anything like cerebral nuance) against you. Your guilty piety because of somebody's pigmentation or choice of sexual partner is a happier form of racism than burning a cross on somebody's lawn, but your hesitation to make judgments based on realities instead of appearances will turn out fatal.

Fags can be fascists and a lot of them are. A poseur the color of anthracite with a safe dry spot in the lifeboat can pass as an albino for the people whose killing he does until he figures out how far the Captain intends to go, then gets tossed overboard to keep the sharks from turning rambunctuous. A woman with the will to betray anybody who gets in her way enjoys brutality as much as men do and gets a bigger rush from power since women seldom get any.

There are never enough seats in the lifeboats and some-body's always getting tossed. It takes a real vampire to stay on board until the end of the voyage. Funny thing is, the sinking liner and the lifeboats are all going to the same place. Nowhere. In other words, exactly where we're going now, and Condoleezza Rice has done America a necessary if depressing service. She has gone that extra mile to push us there. The future will come fast and the end will come quick, thanks to a few fearless Americans like her.

DR. CONDOLEEZZA RICE
Harbinger Of American Neofascism

Paul Robeson, Jr.

Dr. Condoleezza Rice is an articulate and commanding public figure, whose practical task is to translate President George W. Bush's incoherent, ideologically driven, imperial jargon into acceptable and consistent diplomatic language. Apparently, she has no firm ideological or political positions of her own.

Rice's professional background is mainly academic. A brilliant undergraduate at the University of Denver, she earned a bachelor's degree in political science there, obtained her master's degree at the University of Notre Dame, and won her doctorate from the School of International Studies at the University of Denver in 1981. She taught as a distinguished professor of political science at Stanford University and later served as Stanford University's provost for six years, during which she was the institution's chief budget and academic officer.[1]

Rice's career in government began in 1989 in the first Bush administration, in which she was head of Soviet and East European Affairs in the National Security Council until March of 1991. Throughout her tenure in that capacity, she adhered to the ideologically rigid positions of Cold War conservatism. As a result, she was unable to foresee or interpret the great changes that were brought about in the former Soviet Union by Mikhail

Gorbachev. Nevertheless, she was rewarded with fulsome praise and a position as a director of Chevron Corporation. She also served as a board member of the Schwab Corporation and on the international advisory council of J. P. Morgan. When, a decade later, she was appointed to the key post of national security advisor by President George W. Bush, she became the primary person responsible for coordinating the national response to the threat of imminent terrorist attacks.[2]

Rice, however, abdicated from this responsibility. Wedded to a Cold War outlook, she removed the tasks of guaranteeing the full exchange of information between intelligence agencies and of connecting the intelligence dots from the list of national security advisor responsibilities. She essentially reduced the National Security Council to a coordinating body for foreign policy. Since this task is one of the chief responsibilities of the secretary of state, Rice was used by President Bush as a counterweight to Colin Powell.

Matters like terrorism within the US were deemed by Rice to be beyond the Council's immediate concern, despite that body's 1947 legal mandate stating that it should concern itself with domestic threats. Rice degraded the position of chief counterterrorism advisor, then occupied by the highly competent Richard Clarke, so that he no longer met directly with the president, vice president and secretaries of defense and state as he had been mandated to do by President Clinton.

From January of 2001 through August of 2001, Clarke sent National Security Adviser Condoleezza Rice a constant stream of requests for a meeting with the Principals Committee or the Cabinet to discuss al Qaeda and Osama bin Laden as the primary terrorist threats to the US homeland. Rice met Clarke's requests with skepticism and delayed response. It was not until April that Clarke got the opportunity to present his case to the deputies committee.

The committee was divided in its response to Clarke.

Paul Wolfowitz, Secretary of Defense Rumsfeld's deputy, dismissed Clarke's arguments, asserting that Iraq's alleged ties to al Qaeda and Saddam Hussein's "weapons of mass destruction" were the administration's main concerns. Clarke sharply rebutted Wolfowitz, stating bluntly that there was no credible substantiation of either an Iraqi–al Qaeda tie or Saddam Hussein's possession of weapons of mass destruction, and that there was a mountain of credible evidence that al Qaeda intended to strike the US homeland in the immediate future.

The former deputy director of the CIA John McLaughlin (who resigned in 2004) and the former deputy secretary of state Richard Armitage (who resigned in 2005) backed Clarke, whereas Steven Hadley, Rice's deputy, suggested a compromise. The Principals Committee would begin by focusing on al Qaeda and then shift to a consideration of other terrorist threats. This compromised proposal was apparently not made seriously. Notwithstanding his unflagging efforts, Clarke did not receive a hearing from the Principals Committee until September 4, 2001, seven months after his first urgent request and one week before September 11.

Clarke briefed Rice aggressively in preparation for the meeting. She could either decide to treat al Qaeda as just a nuisance, as she had been doing, or to act immediately in accordance with the proposition that al Qaeda posed an "existential threat to the American way of life." There was no middle ground. He concluded by urging Rice to put herself in her own shoes when in the very near future al Qaeda had killed hundreds of Americans: "What will you wish then that you had already done."[3] Rice, in typical bureaucratic fashion, made no direct response to Clarke.

At the meeting, Clarke sounded dire alarms, speaking passionately about "the urgency and seriousness of the al Qaeda threat."[4] George Tenet, former director of the CIA (who resigned in 2005), backed Clarke with equal passion. Former secretary of state Colin Powell supported Clarke in his calm but forceful manner, and laid out an aggressive strategy against al Qaeda. No one disagreed. However, Rice, who had convened the meeting and chaired it, adjourned the session before any decisions could be made. The sole practical result was Clarke's assignment to finalize a National Security Presidential Directive on al Qaeda, which was to be sent to Rice for presidential signature.

I believe that Rice's deliberate stonewalling of Clarke's efforts was directly responsible for the Bush Administration's failure to prevent the tragedy of 9/11. Even as late as September 4, 2001, decisive action by the Principals Committee could have prevented all of the hijackings.

Throughout the spring of 2001, Clarke had bombarded Rice and the rest of the National Security Council staff with memos to the effect that al Qaeda was determined to "have hundreds of dead in the streets of America."[5] Having elicited no response, Clarke acted on his own authority during the first week in July.

He convened his Counterterrorism Security Group and instructed all of its agencies to cancel summer vacations and official travel. Each agency was to report anything unusual, no matter how apparently trivial. Clarke personally requested the FBI to send an immediate official warning to 18,000 police departments, asked the Department of State to alert all of its embassies, petitioned the Department of Defense to go to threat condition delta, the highest state of alert, and called for the Navy to move ships out of Bahrain. He requested the Federal Aviation Administration to send another security warning to all airlines and airports and requested special security at the ports of entry. He rejected the idea of a public warning because he had no proof of a planned attack.

Clarke also convened a White House meeting of the senior security officials at the Immigration and Naturalization Service, the Secret Service, the Coast Guard, the Customs and Border Protection, and the Federal Protective Service. This meeting was attended by the top FBI and CIA counterterrorism experts who agreed with Clarke's premises and reported that they believed al Qaeda was preparing something in the US. Clarke appealed to those present to "Schedule overtime, have your terrorist–reaction teams on alert to move fast. Tell me, tell each other, about anything unusual."[6]

However, none of Clarke's requests were heeded during the period between that July meeting and September 11, 2001.

Moreover, the public record confirms that all attempts by lower-level officials to implement Clarke's recommendations were either ignored or suppressed at the top levels of leadership. Clarke himself was isolated within the top level of the Bush administration. Finally, Clarke has implied that if his recommendations had been fully implemented, the 9/11 hijackings could have been prevented. However, he has carefully avoided saying so explicitly, preferring to detail and dramatize the monumental security failures of the Bush administration.[7]

On August 6, 2001, Condoleezza Rice received a Presidential Daily Brief containing an item titled, "Bin Ladin Determined To Strike In US." This item spoke for itself.

> Clandestine, foreign government, and media reports indicate bin Ladin since 1997 has wanted to conduct terrorist attacks in the US. . . . After US missile strikes on his base in Afghanistan in 1998, bin Ladin told followers he wanted to retaliate in Washington.
>
> The millennium plot [to bomb Los Angeles hatched] in Canada in 1999 may have been part of bin Ladin's first serious attempt to implement a terrorist strike in the US. . . . Although bin Ladin has not succeeded, his attacks against the US embassies in Kenya and Tanzania in 1998 demonstrate that he prepares operations years in advance and is not deterred by setbacks. Al Queda members—including some who are US citizens—have resided in or traveled to the US for years, and the group apparently maintains a support structure that could aid attacks.
>
> We have not been able to corroborate some of the more sensational threat reporting . . . . Nevertheless, FBI information . . . indicates patterns of suspicious activity in this country consistent with preparations for hijackings

or other types of attacks, including recent surveillance of federal buildings in New York. The FBI is conducting approximately 70 full field investigations throughout the US that it considers bin Ladin-related. CIA and the FBI are investigating a call to our Embassy in the UAE [United Arab Emirates] in May saying that a group of bin Ladin supporters was in the US planning attacks with explosives.[8]

Given all this information, Rice's repeated assertion that Clarke's briefings "contained no actionable intelligence information" because they did not provide a precise time or place with regard to an attack must be a lie. The memo of August 6, 2001 itself cites 70 separate investigations that the FBI had already launched. As the cabinet member closest to President Bush and as the person primarily responsible for homeland security, Rice was guilty of criminal negligence if she did not pay attention to the document in question. If she did study it and intentionally did nothing, or, still worse, *deliberately* impeded the efforts of others to do something, Rice should be tried for treason.

In any case, the warning about hijacking was not news to counterterrorism officials, the FBI, or the CIA, since 52 warnings about hijacking were issued by the FAA alone in the six months preceding 9/11. Moreover, there had been many explicit warnings, dating back to the 1990s, about the use of hijacked commercial airliners as missiles to attack major national sites.[9]

I believe also that Rice lied about the events of 9/11. On the morning of that fateful day, she was in her office when she was informed that the first hijacked airliner (Flight 11) had hit the North Tower of the World Trade Center at 8:46 a.m. She claimed that she thought: "What an odd accident."[10] This claim is not credible.

By then, the Air Force National Guard Commander, Major General Paul Weaver had already scrambled two F-15 fighters to New York from Otis Air Force Base in Massachusetts at 8:52 a.m. on his own authority after he could get no definitive response from his superiors. One of the pilots, Lieutenant Colonel Timothy Duffy, recalled that he was told before takeoff, "This looks like the real thing." He flew in "full blower" (over 1,875 mph) all the way. It took him just 11 minutes from the time he entered his cockpit to reach the World Trade Center in time to see the second hijacked plane (Flight 175) hit the South Tower at 9:03.

The idea that Rice, the national security adviser, was not explicitly aware of most of this activity by 9 a.m. is not credible. Moreover, at 8:21 a.m. American Airlines flight service manager Michael Woodward received a call from Amy Sweeney, a Flight 11 stewardess, detailing the hijacking of her plane, and immediately passed on the information to Nancy Wyatt, supervisor of pursers at Boston's Logan Airport. Wyatt, in turn, informed American Airlines headquarters. Almost simultaneously, Vanessa Minter, an American Airlines reservations agent in North Carolina, received a call from Fight 11 attendant Betty Ong describing the hijacking. However, the American Airlines officials on the ground did not believe her and did nothing.

Also at 8:21, Boston flight controller Pete Zalewski suspected "something seriously wrong" with Flight 11 and notified his superiors urgently. Other controllers immediately suspected that Flight 11 had been hijacked and told their superiors. Nevertheless, the North American Aerospace Defense Command (NORAD) was not notified.

Note that, if the two fighters scrambled from Otis Air Force Base had been dispatched at, say, 8:25 a.m. instead of 8:52 a.m., they would have had time to reach the World Trade Center at least 10 minutes before the first plane hit the North Tower, and 23 minutes before the second plane hit the South Tower. Consider also the fact that by 8:46 a.m., New York flight controllers suspected that United Airlines Flight 175 had been hijacked. A full 17 minutes remained to expedite F-15 jets in time to intercept the plane before it hit the South Tower at 9:03 a.m.[11]

It strains credulity beyond reasonable limits to believe that the FAA, the top administration at two major airlines, the administrative leadership of a major airport, NORAD, the top leadership of the US Air Force, the leadership of the US intelligence community, and the entire top leadership of the executive branch of the US government were all completely dysfunctional on the same morning. Therefore, I have concluded that a thorough congressional investigation must be conducted to obtain definitive answers to two questions. Did the executive branch deliberately ignore confirmed advance warnings that the 9/11 terrorist attack would occur specifically in the early fall of 2001? Secondly, did the Bush administration deliberately impede efforts by dedicated government officials, which could have prevented 9/11 after the attacks had been set in motion?

The key witness who must be compelled to answer these questions under oath is the current Secretary of State Condoleezza Rice—because she has been a witness to and a participant in the Bush-Cheney criminal conspiracy against the people and in opposition to the Constitution of the United States.

Rice is the cabinet member who was offered up to the 9/11 Commission to testify without the immunity that President Bush had the power to protect her with. She opted to testify publicly under oath and run the risk of an indictment as she faithfully lied to protect the President and Vice President. The latter two held forth together in private without being sworn.

To white America Rice appears regal—the first African-American woman to occupy the exalted position of secretary of state, the third person in the line of succession to the presidency of the United States. Condoleezza Rice also serves as the perfect example of successful affirmative action, confirmation that in today's America any talented African American descended from freedmen, house slaves, or skilled slaves has the opportunity to rise to the top level of wealth, fame, and power. She is supposedly living proof that American-style democracy works.

But to 75 percent of African Americans who are descended from field slaves and identify themselves as Black (with a capital "B"), Rice, a self-proclaimed "Anglophile," is the equivalent of a talented house slave who identifies with her WASP slave master.

She shares nothing in common with us except the color of her skin. She is the loyal servant of our main enemy and chief oppressor.

One might ask as I do, what possible gain could inspire such a monstrous crime attended by such an astronomically high risk? The obvious answer is greed. The Bush administration is run by a gang of upperclass thieves and political thugs who steal billions. For example, Chevron Corporation, for which Rice had previously served as a director, gained a quarter trillion dollars in value during the first three years of the war in Iraq. It is estimated that the top five oil companies saw their reserves rise in value by over 2.363 trillion dollars since 9/11.[12]

The climate of fear blanketing the nation was created by the Bush administration in the wake of 9/11 in order to gain political advantage. A metaphorical war on terror, in addition to quite real wars against Afghanistan and Iraq, were launched on the strength of the false linkage between 9/11 and Saddam Hussein, and the nonexistent weapons of mass destruction allegedly possessed by Hussein.

Rice was one of the main perpetrators of these two big lies, which were pandered to the American public by a propaganda machine more pervasive than those commanded by Hitler and Stalin. Now Rice is hyping yet another big lie that Iraq is the main front in an endless war on terror. In reality, the main goal of the Iraq war is to control Iraq's oil, and the purpose of the war in Afghanistan is to establish permanent strategic military bases with which to threaten Iran to the west, Pakistan to the east, Russia to the north, and China to the northeast.

If this fantasy can be marketed successfully for the next two years, the profits to oil companies, multinational contractors, and other supporters of the Bush administration will reach unimaginable proportions. The present White House cynically calculates that subsequent administrations will have no choice but to clean up the mess left behind.

This is the context within which we must evaluate the post-9/11 remarks by Bush, Rice, and Rumsfeld about the "great opportunities" presented by New York City's tragedy that extinguished almost 3,000 innocent lives. Bush declared that 9/11 provided "a great opportunity." Rumsfeld spoke of "the kind of opportunities World War II offered, to refashion the world." Rice told the senior members of her National Security Council to think about how to "capitalize on these opportunities to fundamentally change the shape of the world."[13]

The September 2002 document titled "The National Security Strategy of the United States of America," written by Rice on behalf of the Bush administration, reveals a similarity to an imperial manifesto that trumpets an intent to dominate the world. It speaks of invoking preemptive war to "deter a threat before it is unleashed" but implies preventive war against any entity with the theoretical capability to unleash a threat. It also threatens Russia and China in not-so-veiled terms: "The President has no intention of allowing any foreign power to catch up with the huge [military] lead the United States has opened up since the fall of the Soviet Union."

On September 20, 2002, the *New York Times* carried a report on Rice's aforementioned strategy paper, and a story on foreign reaction to the document. The item included a quote from German Justice Minister Herta Däubler-Gmelin criticizing Bush's militaristic, super-patriotic rhetoric. She added that, "Bush wants to divert attention from his domestic problems. It's a classic tactic. It's one Hitler also used." Her reply to official US outrage over her comment was notably unapologetic: "I didn't compare the persons Bush and Hitler, but their methods."

She was right. Bush's fear-mongering and demagogic methods, his right-wing constituency, and his shameless lies are reminiscent of the "moderate" faction of the Nazi Party just prior to the pre-Hitler era. Ghetto Blacks, illegal Mexican immigrants, and gays play the counterparts to Jews, Gypsies and gays in Germany during the years that Hitler rose to power. The Confederate battle flag and the song "Dixie" compare with the Swastika and the

"Horst Wessel Song." All that's missing are the brown uniforms, the funny caps, and the Nazi armbands. The potential storm troopers are concealed in blue uniforms.

The Bush–Rice show plays well in many "red" states that are dominated by a WASP ethnic plurality, and where a significant part of the population still prefers any fascist to any communist. Today, most Americans have long forgotten that in 1939 one third of Americans backed Hitler, one third opposed him, and one third were neutral.[14] And in 1943, at the height of the "War Against Fascism," as it was known, thousands of Midwestern factory workers openly said they would rather see a Hitler victory than work next to a "nigger." President Franklin D. Roosevelt had to send in the National Guard to enforce the desegregation of the war plants.[15]

Against this historical background, the 9/11 tragedy offered Bush's right-wing extremists an ideal political weapon with which to capture the Republican Party. The war on terror could be used to establish one-party control of all three branches of government in the wake of a superpatriotic crusade. And Bush's claim that he was spreading democracy across the Middle East in order to secure the homeland against international Islamic fascism could be falsely linked to the epic World War II struggle against Hitler's war machine. This unhistorical demagogy is reminiscent of Joseph Goebbels, Hitler's chief propagandist.

Let us take a close look at Condoleezza Rice's testimony about her immediate response to the news of the 9/11 disaster.

She claims that at about 9 a.m. she telephoned Bush from her office and told him that a twin-engine plane had struck the North Tower of the World Trade Center, and that she had no more information. According to her, he replied, "What a terrible it sounds like a terrible accident." None of this is credible.

As noted above, by the time Rice was initially informed, it was known to many in and out of government that a terrorist attack had occurred. Two fighters had already been scrambled to the World Trade Center by the Air Force National Guard, and one pilot had witnessed the first attack. It is inconceivable that Rice, as national security advisor, was not immediately informed of this, especially since she was readily accessible in her office. Moreover, former CIA Director Tenet had been informed of the attacks at 8:50 a.m. and had suspected immediately that al Qaeda was responsible for the crash. He, or a close aide, would certainly have called Rice immediately.

The president also certainly had this information by the time Rice called him. At 8:55 a.m., upon his arrival at Booker Elementary School in Sarasota, Florida, Bush had been briefed on the first attack by Captain Deborah Loewer, director of the White House Situation Room, who was traveling with him (despite that Bush maintains he learned of the crash at a later time). Loewer had been informed by her deputy in the Situation Room, who had seen a video of the first crash and suspected that it was a terrorist attack.

Bush's comment after he observed the second crash on television was, "There's one terrible pilot."[16] He did not appear to be concerned about the extraordinary loss of life that had been caused by the two crashes.

I believe that Rice lied about the conversation she had that day with Bush. Moreover, as was the case with Bush, Rice showed little concern about the lives lost on 9/11. She was far more concerned with covering up the Bush administration's abject failure to protect the American people.

In her testimony before the 9/11 Commission on April 8, 2004, Rice hid behind an avalanche of arrogant posturing and windy rhetoric. Regarding her conversations with President Bush, she lied repeatedly under oath in order to cover up his total impotence in a crisis: Rice claimed, "Clarke never asked me to brief the President on counterterrorism."

She did not remember whether she discussed the existence of al Qaeda cells in the United States with Bush.

She claimed that she personally requested the FBI to issue three nationwide warnings about terrorist attacks on the homeland.

She repeatedly insisted that there was no absence of vigor in the White House's response to al Qaeda during the Bush administration's first 233 days in office.

Rice also revealed herself to be a heartless bureaucrat, like Bush and Rumsfeld, when she refused to apologize to the families of the 9/11 victims as Clarke had done several weeks earlier. As for government accountability, her contemptible attitude was that everyone was to blame, and therefore no one was to blame.[17]

Condoleezza Rice is a faithful adherent and loyal executor of President George W. Bush's neoconservative foreign policy, which is reminiscent of the Nazi regime of the late 1930s. The first African-American woman to serve as national security advisor to the president and now as secretary of state, she is to George W. Bush what Ulrich Friedrich Wilhelm Joachim von Ribbentrop was to Adolph Hitler, only in blackface.

It was Rice who plunged the dagger handed to her by Bush into the back of Colin Powell, potentially the greatest Secretary of State since General George Catlett Marshall, and shamelessly strutted into his post. As a former academic, she knows only how to interpret her master's wishes, but is utterly untrained and inexperienced in the fine art of international diplomacy. She is simply unqualified to serve as secretary of state.

We Blacks, who are descended from field slaves, are unassimilated into the US civic culture that accommodates the heirs of the WASP slave owners and their Northern Copperhead allies. We are in it but not of it. We view Dr. Rice, who identifies with the heirs of the slave masters who claimed ownership of her house-slave ancestors, as the loyal servant of our chief political enemy. Less than 10 percent of all African-American voters cast ballots for Bush in the last two presidential elections, and his current popularity among African-Americans is down to 4 percent. Rice is touted as a Republican symbol exclusively to influence impressionable white voters. Anyone who believes that she significantly influences Black voters is living in a fantasy world.

On the contrary, Black people are in a position to expose Condoleezza Rice's betrayal of the national interest as she serves the party of racism, reaction, wealth, and war. Moreover, it is high time we expose her dirty secret—her conscious role as propagandist for American neofascism with a not-so-friendly face.

Notes

1. *Biography of Condoleezza Rice*, http://www.whitehouse.gov/nsc/ricebio.html.
2. Greg Palast, *Armed Madhouse*, Dutton, 2006, pp. 89-90; 172-73.
3. Richard Clarke, *Against All Enemies*, Free Press, 2004, p. 237.
4. *Ibid.*, p. 237.
5. *Ibid.*, p. 236.
6. *Ibid.*, p. 236.
7. *Ibid.*, pp. 234-46.
8. *9/11 Commission Report*, updated, with introduction by Thomas H. Kean and Lee H. Hamilton, Barnes & Noble, 2006, pp. 35, 39, 40, 198-214, 255, 257, 263, 264, 343-45; Richard Clarke's testimony before the 9/11 Commission, March 24, 2004; Condoleezza Rice's testimony before the 9/11 Commission, April 8, 2004.
9. *Ibid.*, pp. 255-63.
10. Paul Thompson and the Center for Cooperative Research, *Terror Timeline*, Harper Collins, 2006.
11. *Ibid.*, pp. 349-468.
12. *Armed Madhouse.*
13. *Armed Madhouse*, p. 116.
14. Harold Evans, *The American Century*, Knopf, 1998, pp. 284-96.
15. Philip A. Klinkner with Rogers M. Smith, *The Unsteady March*, University of Chicago Press, 1999, p. 180.
16. *Terror Timeline*, p. 388.
17. *9/11 Commission Report*, p. 101; *The 9/11 Commission Report One Year Later,* July 22, 2005 Congressional Briefing conducted by Rep. Cynthia McKinney in the Cannon House Office Building [complete record of transcripts and written submissions], pp. 40-46, 101-108.

SAY NUCLEAR

Sapphire

"So shut up, already! You fuckin' cow! Moo Moo! Who needs you?" he shouted.

She broke into tears and ran out of the room. Really, fuck her, who did need her?

But instantly he was contrite.

"I'm sorry, Laura. Laura?" Fuck it, he would go find Condi. She was probably in the gym. Yeah, discuss it with her.

"So what's she talkin' about? What are they talkin' about? Laura said it was in the *New York Times* and the *Washington Post*."

"Let's just go through it, Mr. President."

"No, just tell me."

"Say it once."

He spits the word out.

"You're thinking of nuke like—"

"Korea, Iran, World War II, Vietnam—"

"I think you mean Japan," she says.

"Yeah, you always know what I mean."

"So what you're saying is nuke-clear. And it makes a lot of sense to say it that—"

"Just tell me what it is."

"It's new, new, like new, you know socks—anything new, then clear. Like clear out motherfuckers!"

"Is that right?"

"Yeah, you were just putting too much into it. Try it. You know our plan for success, 10 times is good, 20 is better."

"Nuke clear—"

"New, new, like a new car."

"New clear."

"Yes! Again…"

"Nuclear Nuclear Nuclear Nuclear."

"Perfect! Keep going! You don't want to lose it. You got it!"

"Nuclear Nuclear Nuclear Nuclear Nuclear Nuclear Nuclear Nuclear Nuclear Nuclear Nuclear."

"Five more."

"That's enough, Condi. I got it."

"So, what's so hard about five more?"

"I don't want to do five fucking more, OK?"

"OK, Mr. President."

ANOTHER AMERICAN LEGACY

Kate Bornstein

1. Scene One: The Russian Empire at the End of the 19th Century.

14-year-old Anya sets out from Minsk in Poland to rescue 16-year-old Max, the love of her life. She's alone and on foot. Max is worse off. He'd been speaking out in support of the Reds, and the Czar's White Russian troops have taken him to Siberia for internment in one of their notorious work camps. Anya has no money for this months-long journey, but she can sing. So she sings for her supper. Stopping at farmhouses, taverns and inns along the way, she offers her sweet voice in return for food and lodging. Sometimes she gets paid in cash. (Two decades later, Anya would sing solo from the great stage at Carnegie Hall, as a member of a choir of immigrant Russians who'd settled in northern New Jersey to work the family silk mills.) Anya's journey crosses 11 time zones, and by the time she arrives at the Siberian camp, she has enough money to pay two guards to turn their heads as Max slips out under the wire and joins her in the woods outside the camp. Together, they make the arduous journey on foot, all the way back across Russia and Poland—wolves nipping at their heels—barely evading starvation and marauders—to Germany where a cargo ship is waiting to take them to America, paid for by relatives who have settled there.

Well, they made it. I'm living proof. Anya and Max were my father's parents. I attribute certain values of mine to this heritage: risking everything for love and freedom, breaking away from and speaking out against tyranny and injustice.

2. Scene Two: Civil War Era Alabama, on a Plantation near Clinton in Greene County.

Behind the main house, hundreds of acres of cotton rise from the dark clay soil that gives the region its name, The Black Belt. As darkness falls, a sense of urgency permeates the buildings. Inside the master's house, slave house servants search for places to hide the silver and other valuables. Outside, male slaves scramble to hide stores of food. For the past week, word has spread like wildfire through the county that Union soldiers are nearby, sacking homes and stealing everything in sight. Battles over the Tennessee River Valley, just 150 miles to the north, have rumbled for months as both sides fight to claim control of the superhighway of the South. From time to time, stories of atrocities inflicted upon families and slaves by the federal troops filtered through the slave quarters and the main house. A young woman, Julia, daughter of the white plantation owner and one of his black house slaves, follows her father's orders and rounds up the family's horses, moving them from the barn to a hiding place that only she knows . . .

The story of Julia, great-grandmother of Dr. Condoleezza Rice, opens a chapter called "American Legacy" in the book *Condoleezza: The Condoleezza Rice Story*, by Antonia Felix (New Market, 2005). The biographer goes on to say that this story was handed down generation to generation as Rice family lore. Like all legends, family or otherwise, there are many lessons to be gleaned from them, many ways to interpret their meaning for future generations.

Clearly, Condoleeza learned that when there is enough fear of attack by outsiders, the correct response—maybe even the noble response—is to defend her master's house.

3. Writing this essay, I decided to do some research into my family history. Here's what I learned about Max: He was actually a white Russian, defending his property and cash, and protecting the Czar against the Bolshevik revolutionaries. And while Anya did in fact sing a solo at Carnegie Hall, it was in large part because her family was well-off and they could afford her opera lessons. What's more, it looks like Anya preceded Max to America by two years. There were no Siberian camps, no arrests. In fact, they had an arranged marriage, and disliked each other intensely from the day they met until the day they died. The longer he could stay away from her, the better. The part about escaping through the Siberian forests with wolves nipping at their heels was true, it turns out, but it was my cousin Davy and his brother, and no one really knows from whom they were running.

I also learned that no one else in my family had constructed this particular family lore. What happened? Am I delusional? Is this other version correct? Does every version reveal some truth, even if that truth tells us more about the present than the past? Does each story let us know mostly about the person who constructed it?

I first heard my grandma's tale as a young boy. I could have sworn that's how the Bornstein line was explained to me. But I can also imagine myself wondering what it was like to be a young girl alone in Russia, out on the road, madly in love, singing for her supper. Maybe that's what I made up one evening as I lay in bed, trying to take my mind off feeling like the freak that I was for wanting to be a girl in a world that said wanting that was perverted, a sin against God.

Growing up, we learn to lie about who we are for all different reasons. So that no one locks us up. So that we don't get beat up. We lie about our histories to sustain the illusion that we've got some power over the course of our lives. That's how family legacies are born. Some of us rewrite our legacies so that the reality doesn't kill us. As we retell it, we become part of it. It makes our choices relevant. In keeping with the legacy of my revolutionary grandparents, I'm doing my very best to raise hell against American dominant culture.

4. Condoleezza's biographer states that this story about the Rice family—this American legacy—was handed down generation to generation. But isn't it Condoleezza's version? Clearly, Condoleeza's legacy needs an overhaul. Americans can no longer afford for her to believe in this version. No American legacy is worth weaving into the future if it permits the continued institutionalization of violence, fear, and oppression.

Condoleezza Rice could interpret her family history in many ways. She could perpetuate a value system that runs in her family—to behave honorably and bravely against those who inspire violence and hatred, rather than in the service of the dominant and the self-righteous. She could rewrite that family history to have a very different outcome. Instead of protecting the master's house when it's under siege, she could understand that the whole system at work ("you're either with us or against us") is a trap. She could redirect all that loyalty and honor to protect the underclass, to protect the true people at risk. She could burn that house down.

IMAGINING CONDI, OR THE RISE
OF THE BLACK SUPERHUMAN

Wanda Coleman

"In the world of men, strive to be a man." (Jewish folk saying)

Miss Lady's swift stride through the halls of government causes heads to nod. Her scent is feminine but not feline, although she has gristle—a lean and muscular body, an athletic build. She has maintained her weight a few pounds under-average, for occasions when she might wish to engage in the high-caloric. She has a worldwide team of experts at the bitten nail tips of her Chief Aide. Her instructions are terse and emphatic. Her staff is the terror of the photocopy room and commissary.

Note 1: Anyone acquainted with the Black urban underclass has checked the frequency with which the gender line is symbolically violated or becomes a nonissue, as those trapped in it reinvent themselves. Hip lingo becomes a rich ghetto vernacular rife with coinage (from muthafatha to manwoman). In its post-Civil-Rights Era re-subjugation of Blacks (via corporate tyranny, population control via unmonitored immigration, the "deballing" of the Equal Employment Opportunity Commission (EEOC) and the under-mining or neutering of other important legislation), an anti-intel-lectual and profoundly racist America II has continued to foist its peculiar socioeconomic role reversals upon the slavery-rooted subculture. Black men must be unthreatening, if not effeminate, in appearance and demeanor, since we are all being judged by "the content our characters," as Martin Luther King, Jr. has noted. However, we women, in the name of survival (no matter how ineffectual that survival may be), are allowed to adapt personality traits that imbue us with an oft-considered masculine quality identified with power and force of character. In a bizarre twist on the Hebrew saying, "in the world of men strive to be a man," the urban African-American female, regardless of origin, finds herself striving toward, if not always achieving, this "otherly" directive. The lofty achievements of Condoleezza Rice warrant a moment to bear witness to one of "our" remarkable exceptions.

She has a half-dozen lifestyle rituals: church as often as possible (any denomination); regular exercise on the job and in between, and while on the go if necessary; and a tri-annual review of her personal goals, a reassessment of those obtained, and an analysis of how close she has come to attaining others. This is information she will occasionally share with close friends or relatives in lieu of small talk. She derives a thrill in discovering a vulnerable political underbelly in flagrante delicto.

Note 2: Condoleezza exemplifies this rare, omnivorous breed of warped individualist, more inclined to be intelligent as opposed to "intellectual," a departure from the normative if formed under similar social stresses. While having high IQs, they almost always without exception have no creative quotient (CQ). They are great exceptions, but they are never geniuses in the true meaning of that oft-abused word. Hence, they are most likely to succeed in people-oriented professions in which they might control or affect the destinies of others. Artists, musicians, and poets are mysteries to them: innovators they admire on one hand and detest on the other. Often they do not like movies of any kind, dislike most if not all Black styles of music (declaring defensively that music has no race). They do respect authority; therefore, attorneys, criminologists, educators, historians, philosophers, politicians, religious leaders, and those who engage in the physical sciences matter, and often matter supremely. They are, circumstantially, in this bizarre fashion, Nietzsche's *Übermenschen*: superbly self-sufficient, super-individualists trained, in one way or another, to withstand the relentless cruelties of American racism.

She knew all the dances at one time in her youth, but now operates on such lofty levels that nostalgia has become a luxury. When it comes to music, whatever plays outside a concert hall, she prefers "universal" midrange melodic compositions, preferably classical, that lilt in the background, or at the edge of consciousness and do not interfere with conversations, impose difficult moods, or evoke difficult memories.

Note 3: At critical moments in the shaping of their identities, the Black Superhumans may have been aided and encouraged by other such individuals passing in order to survive in the White World. This kind of getting by does not refer to skin color but to temperament. Chameleons by circumstance, these are usually mentored by native-born Blacks, or immigrant men of color, who have learned to suppress their gifts and not draw attention to themselves for any reason outside advancement. They believe the future is theirs to shape for others. Their purpose is to be left unmolested as they do what they must among those they regard as inferiors, and/or do whatever they can get away with without being "made." They select friends carefully and often. When they recognize a kindred spark in a younger individual, they will take measured steps to foster it in some manner, directly or indirectly. They love and will sacrifice for their protégés, as they might have had or wanted love and sacrifice for themselves.

Her confidence is reinforced by the evidence that few are capable of damaging or dispatching her. Unlike those who are awed, intimidated, or oppressed by the weighty job responsibilities comprising such lofty roles as national security advisor and secretary of state, she is comfortable since she always thrives when challenged. Often she is the brainy architect who concocts the strategy that salvages an administrative gaff or goof. In assuming these dynamic roles, she has imbued them with the elusive "safeness," which grows out of an inevitable overlay of the quiescent "mammy" stereotype (who could always salvage a white child, but never her own) even as she reinvents it for all time—except that she is a Vashti instead of a Beulah.

Note 4: The Black Superhumans neutralize and stymie cries of racism the instant they appear. They are men and women literally steeled against racist forces. If they can survive an oft-subtle, lifelong economic assault on their psyches and souls, they can withstand anything any fragment of America has to throw at them. As such, they walk over the waters of controversy like Jesus Christ. No one is capable of impugning their integrity because it simply cannot be impugned. Those who have the money to consult with authority and make use of the wisdom and judgments of others will do so. Conservative in their lifestyles, their old habits take root. They are more likely to be tight-fisted after running tight ships. If and when they attain the power sought, or any modicum of it, they will seldom use or apply it "to help poor Black people" (be they survivors of acts of God, or simply survivors), content largely in having acquired such power, to enjoy the side benefits: celebrity, recognition, wealth. Although they may engage in philanthropic pursuits, they generally shy away from the notion of belonging to a group, even a group of such like super-personalities, and especially a group of weak-willed, mushy-brained (as they would see it) African Americans. Their unusual appetites for power are accompanied by a militaristic respect for power, and they usually despise anything they perceive as effete, ineffectual, or weak.

She has had musical training, could not excel at it creatively, but still enjoys the therapeutic value in playing the piano, entertaining friends, surprising an official or amusing royalty. When it comes to art, she loves Romare Bearden and Jacob Lawrence, but hasn't kept up. Poetry is avoided because it brings back unpleasant encounters with boys who, whenever she dropped something, say school books, left them on the ground, refusing to help her pick them up unless collared by an instructor. She enjoys the biographies of rich and famous men. She will make time for a good novel and the occasional memoir with credible, amazing, uplifting and inspirational plot lines.

Note 5: One of the major shames of the 20th century was the failure of our nation to take full responsibility for slavery, and its inhumane residuals in contemporary American life. What it has wrought, in confusion and complexity, among Black men and women remains a tragedy and a travesty. And very much discussed. Because slavery was also an economic tool, the descendants of slaves have developed a remarkable sensitivity to the whims of private financial fortunes and markets, as well as public finances and revenues beyond the sheer force of an oppressive poverty. Our bloodlines are other people's moneylines. Any significant change in the fiscal structure of the nation is felt first "on bottom," somewhere in African-American quarters: hence, the strength and power of Black male sexuality when its repressed masculinity is channeled into the music, dance, fashion, and other arts. However, this is accompanied by a twin circumstance, which is an extension of what Dr. Frances Cress Welsing calls, in effect, the emasculation of our men and the defeminization of our women. That is to say, that the nature of white oppression has not only warped and reshaped our language, it has warped and reshaped the psyches of those of us who lack the strength of character, moral fortitude, or familial and/or social support to resist its devastating and very real consequences (drug and alcohol abuse, gang violence, homelessness, conflicts with the law, prostitution, and life-taking STDs). The ultimate crisis in 21st-century America is that racism continues to turn as many of our Black men into de facto women as possible by sending them to prison rather than college, and by seeing to it that our Black women become de facto men in their stead, in order to survive. The organic and oft-deliberate development and encouragement of the Black Superhuman by the cultural movers of the 1960s has been the most effective counterstrategy in combating these twin devils of American racism.

She is tastefully, immaculately, and primly dressed; not a hair or thread out of place. There are smiles, some distant and pro forma, others genuinely warm. She is always gracious, minds her Ps & Qs, and speaks in pleasant, no-nonsense stentorian tones, which, if called for, neatly soften into an intimacy that never exists. She's an orator, certainly, even if she cannot carry a tune. She has dated professional men always, but the higher she climbs the scarcer the single brothers; and, statistically she understands that professional men don't choose Black women for mates.

Note 6: Ideally, the Black Superhuman is able to recognize his or herself somewhere in the course of his or her unorthodox education, and may actually assist by seeking out mentors. This education usually comes as a jagged gestalt; that is, several high-powered individuals channeling their energies into a protégé at differing moments throughout his or her youth. One might assume that such learning starts with one or both parents, as it often does. However, close relatives, godparents, clergymen, teachers, neighbors, and community leaders may also take part in the edification and illumination processes. The protégé is often subjected to harsh lessons about the importance of such qualities as self-discipline, honor, integrity, etc., accompanied by religious instruction. In a very real sense, they are The Chosen, or DuBois' Talented Tenth. As such, they are presented with the glittering remains of all possible worlds: that is, the hopes, dreams and aspirations of the mentors who school them. They will be made privy to certain workings of the White World, and will be taught how to defend themselves against it, and how to remain self-possessed while so doing. Yet, as they learn, and the more they learn, the greater the danger that a protégé is likely to develop contempt and disgust for those "undeserving" lessers, who will be considered intellectual, moral, or spiritual inferiors. Essentially trapped within the Black underclass, a protégé may initially despise those around them, yet develop a deep shame and self-loathing. Also, what goes on in the Black underclass may no longer interest them unless it can further their escape from it, into the upper echelons of the larger culture (to cover the Black with "the green"), to operate as an individual, free, they think, of the artifice and onus of race.

Yet, she has been described as "not the marrying kind," and "unable to find a man who isn't competitive." (She would sooner see her own throat cut, while in neon-orange coveralls, than lose her gazillion federal security ranking.) Rather, it is too late to change behavior she prefers, and which has proven itself in rewards and accolades beyond all childhood hopes. Her climb has been too effing arduous and lucrative to give it up for anyone who could not match her step by step, rung for rung. Too, it is too late to have children, and she believes that all regret is a waste; it is another reason why she has maintained her teeth and figure so well, to the envy of her frumpy bureaucratic sisters.

Note 7: As parasitic as their existences may appear to their liberal counterparts, to dismiss these unclassifiable individuals solely as parasites is a mistake, and can be dangerous once they have assumed positions of power. These individuals are "true" believers (in themselves, if not God or Allah), and they thrive on the racist fear, hatred, and warped individualism inherent in even the most casual acquaintance with a native-born white person. Often, Black Superhumans allow themselves to be used (by any group in power) to create the illusion of a level socioeconomic playing field, as has Justice Clarence Thomas, as did ex-Republican Julius Caesar Watts, Jr, as did O.J. Simpson and Rosey Grier. They may or may not openly declare allegiance to one party or another, one group or another; but this is essentially a moot point. They are difficult to attack on either the right or the left because they exemplify and embody the American myth of life, liberty, and the pursuit of happiness. They have achieved success. They are beholden to no one except themselves, having pulled themselves up by humble bootstraps. Therefore their only true allegiance is to themselves (and their mentors, if modest) as superior individuals, who made supreme efforts. When healthy, they have no qualms about confronting bigotry (like Watts); but otherwise, they remain silent and conduct themselves in a predictable and defensive fashion (like Thomas). Secure in that root belief, ensconced in a self-congratulatory smugness, they feel doubly assured, and are able to pass freely among virtually any group, even feigning agreement and activism, common interests, commitment, and involvement when necessary, if necessary.

*She has a slight gap between her two front teeth, which make them "happy teeth,"
and she is sensitive about them, a fact she has hypnotized herself to never reveal.
As a child she was called "rabbit face," "evil beaver," "buck-toothed," and dirty
appellations that still make the teen inside her turn deep chocolate. When she
confronts the mirror these days, she shines those pearls and grins ear to ear, knowing she is accepted and respected in places her ex-classmates could not imagine, let
alone gain entry. Condi hates the smell of vapor rubs and cocoa butter almost as
much as she hates telling anecdotes.*

Note 8: The Black Superhuman will do little to nothing to create or encourage a true open society for native-born American
Blacks. Theirs is a self-hatred that turns upon itself pathetically.
They are particularly anxious to see that any legislation designed
to empower the rest of a disenfranchised African America fails or
is neutered, or gutted of enforcement powers. Once they enter the
halls of power, they become dependent and parasitic upon what
they perceive as the failures of the Negro Race. While they oft
do nothing, having settled into "having gotten there," they tacitly
agree that the numbers of Blacks who excel in academic studies or
in the white-collar professional classes must be kept at a minimum.
Otherwise, opportunities to stand out or be special will be rarer if
there are hundreds of Black Superhumans around. (If professional
basketball is any example, that is not necessarily the case.) Such
a society in which African Americans of slave origin could truly
thrive would mean devising mechanisms to release the repressed
energies of a subculture, virtually at once, on four levels of government. It would mean creating a rush of patriotic Afro-American
energy, immensely constructive (in ultimately relieving all subcul-
tures of racism) for our nation in that all African Americans might,
as the saying goes, "seek their own social levels." There would be,
without a doubt, a reshuffling of the racial hierarchy or pecking order. For the first time in American history, the reprehensibly shady
legal (and criminal-justice) restraints would be off. Mitigating fac-
tors and extenuating circumstances would not be circumscribed
by political doubletalk and hijinks, and the language of freedom
would be clearly spoken. Under such liberated conditions, within

a generation or two, the Black Superhuman would appear virtually commonplace. This would be for the good of the entire nation.

At night when she retires, after a massage and bath if there's time, she's so exhausted sex is seldom an issue. She is not driven by desire, only power, and having power sates her every craving, except for that of more power. Of course she's had a bit of experience, but those interlockings have never amounted to anything sufficiently substantive, certainly not creating the kinds of sensations that spark strong interest and urges for the repeat experience. Whether someone was too big or not big enough was never at issue. Nor was oral flickability. Whatever they were, they were not right, and therefore, she found consolation in focusing upon her mundane pursuits. Inspiration, desire, romance—such words sounded the concerns of fools, dreamers, and misfits.

Note 9: Ironically, it is not uncommon for Black Superhumans to engage in self-hatred. They hate themselves not only because they have African blood, but because that blood has affected their appearance, and they may believe they do not meet the standards of beauty highly prized in the dominant culture. When they are ugly, they do their best to mitigate that ugliness by cultivating charm, cuddliness, or wittiness. At their most psychotic, they would obliterate the entire Black race, especially those of us who are native-born African Americans, and leave only themselves standing in some cases, perhaps along with a few of the brighter-skinned of the Black Diaspora's new arrivals. In other cases, they would extinguish themselves as well, thus fulfilling the dicta of Huey P. Newton, whose return to street life, as the Civil Rights and Black Power Movements waned, ironically answered his eleventh-hour call for "Revolutionary Suicide."

Today, as Miss Lady strolls the halls headed for the press conference, meeting room, floor of the Senate, floor of the House—the inner sanctum—she exudes the juices of presidential power and the authority with which she has been endowed. She radiates the orgasmic power she derives from this feeling, and is very much a lightning rod of sorts, transmitting it via a quiet thrill to all who come in contact with this glowing being, this resplendent example of her race. She bristles with it, head set straight, chin up, shoulders squared. Absolutely fearless. Her rightful place in history is beyond reproach or excision. This is the psycho-bitch, a praise that defies gender. Be grateful that she is not a soldier, even if she is a killer in her own right. She is what happens when the homicide–suicide impulse is highly controlled. If you do not kowtow properly, she will have your job tonight and your scalp in the morning.

Condi as Carousel Ride, Sue Coe

Timeline, Kara Walker

Rice, Jason Mecier

THE LITTLE GIRL WHO LOST HER COLOR AND BECAME PRESIDENT

Faith Ringgold

During the most tumultuous time in American history, a precious little Black girl named Condi was born in a town called Bombingham, in the deep, deep South. Condi's mother was a teacher and her father was a Presbyterian minister of his own church. They had vowed that though Condi could not have a hamburger at Woolworth's, or sit in the front of the bus, she would be educated and she could be President of the United States.

Condi was beautiful and smart and her mother and father gave her every advantage in life: ballet, piano, ice skating, and French lessons as well as support for an undergraduate, graduate and post-graduate university education. Condi's parents were evangelists of education and Condi was a perfect student.

She could play Chopin, Beethoven, and Brahms and speak fluent French, Spanish, and Russian. Condi was educated.

Condi was taught to ignore racial discrimination. She was taught not to worry about the "small slights" of "whites only" signs in public pools, movie houses and department store dressing rooms; for she was educated and could be—indeed would be—President of the United States.

The town of Bombingham had been so named because of the many bombings of the homes of Black people who had moved into white neighborhoods. One year there had been so many bombings that the sky turned black with smoke and the sun refused to shine for several days.

It was during this period of intense bombings that four little Black girls were killed in a church. Condi was in Sunday school in her father's church, not far away from where the four little girls were killed. Condi knew one of the girls who was killed. She was Condi's age.

The Black people mourned the death of their children. A movement of peaceful marches and demonstrations were organized to protest the killing of innocent Black men, women and children. It had all begun when Rosa Parks, the mother of the Civil Rights Movement refused to give up her seat to a white man and inspired Martin Luther King, Jr. to lead the Montgomery bus boycott. The struggle for equality and freedom in America was on.

The Ku Klux Klan came after the Black people and set fire to their homes and lynched them. And the police set police dogs upon the peaceful demonstrators and forced them back with water hoses. The entire nation was embroiled in this massive struggle against racial hatred of Black people, this unequal treatment, this "Second Civil War."

But Condi's father was not a "marching in the street preacher." Condi was perched high up on her father's shoulders when she saw the wreckage of the bombings and the brave souls who marched peacefully against the snarling police dogs and water hoses to protest the killing of the four little Black girls who died in the bombing in Bombingham.

Condi was changed. Some say the change came when the four little Black girls were killed in the church bombing in Bombingham.

No one knows exactly when or how it happened

But it was clear that—although Condi, from all outside appearances, still looked like a little Black girl—Condi was not Black or colored or Negro as Black people were called in those days; nor was she a Coon, a Darkie, or a Nigger. She was educated. And she had been taught by her parents to ignore all acts of racial discrimination. For though she could not eat at the lunch counter or sit in the front of the bus or go to school with white children, she could be, and indeed would be, President of the United States.

There have always been Black people who from outward appearances "look black" but have suppressed their Black culture in order to gain acceptance in the "white world." You might call this a kind of human sacrifice but more of the soul than the body. The Black body remains intact but the soul is denied, diminished, given up, sacrificed, so as not to run interference with, or, in a desperate attempt to blend in with white people, their culture and politics.

Black culture is a complex combination of color, class, and nationality. On the one hand there is the cool attitude, the hip gait and the stride, the hip lingo, the bebop and the hip hop, the dancers and the dancing, the music and the songs, the singers and the singing, the speakers and the speaking, the teachers and the teachings, the sense of humor, the stories and the storying, and the laughing Black people love so much—the loud laughing of Black people at Black people themselves.

On the other hand there are those Black people born to waste away in the struggle for a minimum level of existence in a cold white world. Some Black people are born with gifts of great promise but none can take success for granted without a struggle. Some have been born with the privilege of an education, others with the determination and the support to struggle for one. But none have been born with equal opportunity without an intense sustained struggle. Still others go through life trying to find out "was happening?" with varying measures of success.

When James Brown screams "I'm a Soul Man!" he is telling us he's a Blackman—as if we can't see. When Aretha sings "All I want is a little R-E-S-P-E-C-T when I get home" she is echoing a Black woman's major concern. Through the power and universality of his and her Black music we see and hear both of them!

To many Black people a loss of color is cause for a funeral, a mass burial, at which centuries of a glorious Black history and culture, dating back to the first human being born in Ethiopia, is buried and forgotten. A loss of Blackness is a cause for deep mourning.

But still there are Black people who lose their color. These Black people voted for Condi for president in large numbers. Other Black people, caught in the middle of "the first woman and the first Black president," closed their eyes, bowed their heads and walked into the voting booths. Still others stayed home and hoped for, prayed for, the best.

Well, as the story goes, Condi, the little Black girl who had been born Black in Bombingham but was not Black, colored or Negro, nor was she a Coon, Darkie, or Nigger. She could speak fluent French, Spanish, and Russian. She had wanted to be a classical pianist and played Brahms, Beethoven, and Chopin, and became a scholar of Soviet Russian politics and culture and advised the President of the United States on Russian affairs. And later advised his son, who also became President of the United States.

She was indeed educated and could be—would be—and indeed was now—(as was predicted by her parents some fifty-four years before at her birth in the town of Bombingham)—president of the United States.

On the night before the presidential inauguration, Condi had a dream in which she was alone in a church, not her father's Presbyterian church, but a Baptist church. There was smoke everywhere. She heard children screaming for help in the next room. Condi tried to reach the children as several men draped in white hoods fled past her out the door of the burning church. She thought of following the hooded men to safety when the children's screams for help forced her to stay.

The children were trying to tell her something and in her dream they were trying to show her something too, but it was so dark and smoky and, as dreams will be, she was unsure of where they were, or what language they were speaking. Finally there was silence and the smoke cleared and the children were now in the same room with her. She reached out to touch them and they disappeared. Only four little dresses, the kind little girls wear to Sunday school, remained. The dresses were burned black and lying on the floor. They got up off the floor and walked away as if someone was wearing them. But no one was. Condi woke up. She had had that dream before but never was it so startling and so clear.

So how was Condi on her first day of being President Condi of the United States of America? Had she exercised, as was her habit, to the music of Led Zeppelin, and had she played Brahms, Beethoven, and Chopin on her new piano at the White House? And what does she have to tell us now that she has the power to speak, not as an adviser to the most powerful president in the world but as that most powerful leader herself?

Meanwhile, from the presidential suite, we heard the sounds of piano playing not Brahms, Beethoven, or Chopin but Duke Ellington's ingenious piano arrangement of "Satin Doll" played with the jazz virtuosity of the master himself.

Outside on the White House lawn, the reporters and photographers from all over the world were gathering. It was just minutes until we would hear a message that could change the course of events in the world for the next decade.

A tall, slim woman walked up and stood in the shadows. She appeared to be ready to make an entrance. Security was exceptionally high. Anticipation was at its breaking point.

"And now the 44th President of the United States, President Condoleezza Rice."

There were audible gasps as President Condi, elegantly clothed in a Kente cloth suit and head-wrap with luscious strings of gold and amber beads around her neck approached the presidential podium. There was a deafening applause and at the same time several groups of angry people, arms flailing and jabbering inaudibly, had to be restrained from approaching the rostrum and forcibly removed from the room.

Could this be the new President Condi?

As she opened her mouth to speak the place went wild. The former president, his father, mother and wife fainted and had to be carried out bodily.

By that time I left (the end).

IDENTITY OVER POLITICS

Rachel Holmes

Condoleezza Rice likes to point out frequently that in America it took nearly a century to end slavery, that women didn't get the right to vote until the early 20th century, and that Black people didn't get full voting rights until 1965. In fact, America's first Black female secretary of state spends as much time talking about race, sex, and gender, and rights-based politics as the average postmodern feminist academic. Does Rice's oft-stated commitment to promoting the rights of women and Black people translate into policy and action, or is this centerpiece of her style merely political expedience and hypocrisy? And what does her use of the language of identity and difference indicate about the limitations and dangers of the use of identity politics in US domestic and international policy?

　　　Rice never fails to miss an opportunity to locate herself as a racialized, sexualized subject, a habit developed when she was a Stanford academic teaching political science in the 1980s. Consider this remark from 1983, three years after she had changed her political allegiance from Democratic to Republican, and three years before she had her first hands-on experience of government:

The understanding of arms control, the respective views and needs of all the nations, is fundamental to our very existence. Blacks should be part of this understanding, as they should be in every other field of American thought and progress. It would be a shame to leave such a vital national concern in the hands of white males over forty![1]

Talking about identity and difference has consistently remained part of Rice's rhetorical style, both as national security advisor and as secretary of state. Accepting the Woman of Valor Award from the Independent Women's Forum in May 2006, she returned to her familiar theme:

Our founding fathers, trying to create a perfect union for we the people, couldn't quite find a way to deal with slavery. And so instead, they left my ancestors to be three-fifths of a man [sic]. But some hundred plus years later, I stand before you as a descendent of those people who were three-fifths of a man [sic] and I ask, Would anybody have thought it possible?[2]

Since Rice's rise to power and celebrity in the spotlight of global politics and international diplomacy, there has been no end of weak-minded analysis and debate from both centrist liberal social feminists and opportunistic antifeminist reactionaries about what she represents with respect to antiracism and feminism.

Self-disciplined, demure, and steely, Rice is the hot-house child of conscientious, doting, ambitious, overprotective middle-class parents who dedicated themselves to fostering her boundless self-confidence and not leaving her feeling angry or inferior. Figure skater, accomplished concert-standard pianist, diligent academic, Rice has been breaking career precedents for Black women in American government throughout her formidable career, but the methods of her route to power and achievement remain as old and familiar as patriarchy itself. True to her name, derived from the Italian *con dolcezza*, renaissance woman Rice has fashioned herself with the assiduous sweetness of chaste, conventional, sexually modest, Christian femininity. Like England's virgin Queen Elizabeth I, who painted herself Madonna-white to posit her iconic power and divine right, Rice has presented herself as married to God, state, and nation, and thus unavailable to any mortal man. For even a hope of a shot at intimacy, a man for Rice must be the President of the United States.

It's the oldest trick in the book. Men—and women who imitate them—want her around because of her much-vaunted sexual unavailability, because she toes the line, and because she is, ultimately, unthreatening in her social and personal behavior. The media are readily supplied with lifestyle stories about Rice's reassuringly feminine foible: an addiction to Ferragamo shoes, diet tips, and dedication to her workout routine. Rice's official image is founded on an irreconcilable contradiction. As a Black woman in high political office, she represents herself, and is represented, as challenging—perhaps even subverting—traditional institutional inequalities. In truth, her validation and power depend upon her active repetition of this dominant culture and its value system. Rice's distinguished office is not the result of democratic process or Black self-determination: she was chosen by Bush, not voters.

Rice's deployment of the rhetoric of identity and difference supports her personal advancement and competitive desire to win. Tough as nails but always melodious, never-strident Condoleezza is a career academic and politician who has seized whatever she can to oil the wheels of ruthless and unfettered ambition. She wields the apparatus of hetero-normative sexuality and a fairly conventional, narrow-ranging intellectualism to win approval and power. Her purported sexual ambivalence is part of the package for her boy patrons, not a potential wildcard; Condoleezza the maybe-lesbian merely adds a cherry topping to the heady cocktail presented by her repressed sexuality and unfettered power. Irrespective of her sexuality, her propagation and support for virulently homophobic policy at home and abroad make clear her politics on sexual rights and freedoms.

Rice is not alone amongst African Americans whose racial identity has been positioned as central to their progress in right-wing US politics. She keeps close company with Clarence Thomas, formerly tainted by allegations of sexual harassment, now a conservative on the Supreme Court, and Colin Powell, who made his reputation in the first Gulf War and lied to the UN about WMDs to justify the Iraq war. Cautious Black activists of a new generation clear-sightedly probe and analyze attacks on Rice from both left and right as possible reflections and justifications of a racist society that isolates and thus neutralizes high-achieving Black individuals. However, Rice is not politically and culturally misguided because she is Black, nor because she is a woman: she is politically and culturally misguided because she is a militarist neoconservative who formulates, propagates, supports, and defends US political and cultural-free market capitalist imperialism. Kenyon Farrow raises an issue: "While I disagree with most of her choices politically and personally, I also understand that America offers Black people very few options, and she has chosen one of the few options we have to ensure her personal survival. What other options has America offered a genius Black girl born in 1950s Birmingham, Alabama?"[3] One answer to Kenyon's question is represented by a genius Black girl born a decade before Rice in 1940s Birmingham, Alabama: Angela Davis, who knows what it is like to be persecuted for political belief in freedom, what it is like to be inside an American jail, and what it means to choose ethics and the struggle for economic and social justice over personal advancement. Rice represents the most reactionary segment of the Bush administration. It is extremely dangerous to pretend that terrorism makes it necessary for the state to deprive its citizens of their rights, and that the United States should ignore whole volumes of international law.[4]

We now know enough about Rice's track record to evaluate her on her actions rather than her rhetoric, and therefore to know that her lip service to the ethics of racial and sexual justice and equality are exactly that. Since 2001, Rice has presided over, and promoted, the evangelical unilateralism of US foreign policy and its escalating lawlessness. The Patriot Act, extraordinary extradition, the rejection of UN criticism of the Guantanamo detention center, the refusal to declare what occurred at the Abu Ghraib prison as torture, the argument that the Geneva Conventions of 1949 do not apply to the insidiously named war on terrorism—these are the positions and policies she has propagated since 2001.

Since its launch in 2004, Rice has also consistently supported the President's Emergency Plan for AIDS Relief (PEPFAR), the President's five-year, supposedly $15-billion program that channels funding for HIV/AIDS, tuberculosis, and malaria primarily to 14 target countries: Botswana, Cote d'Ivoire, Ethiopia, Guyana, Haiti, Kenya, Mozambique, Namibia, Nigeria, Rwanda, South Africa, Tanzania, Uganda, and Zambia. In his annual State of the Union address in January 2003, President Bush announced the provision of an additional $10 billion to AIDS programs in Africa and the Caribbean, which should have brought to $15 billion the US government's total commitment to the cause following a $5 billion allocation under the Clinton administration that had yet to be disbursed. A relatively small portion of the Bush administration's pledge, just $1 billion over five years, was intended for the Global Fund for AIDS, Tuberculosis and Malaria (GFATM). The US Congress eventually appropriated $2.4 billion in 2004, and the total amount released was just $350 million. The total amount of US aid money for 2004 was $17.55 billion; the military budget approved for 2004 was $368.2 billion, excluding the additional $87 billion war supplemental requested by the Bush administration. This military budget was for fighting the so-called war on terror and to sustain the occupation of Iraq.

PEPFAR's globally applied criteria are that it will provide no funding to any organization that distributes condoms or supports abortion. PEPFAR will not provide money to any organizations that talk openly of working with lesbian and gay groups or sex workers. PEPFAR will not provide money to any organization that does not promote sexual abstinence as the centerpiece of its strategy to combat AIDS. Rice describes PEPFAR as "transformational diplomacy in action," actively supporting PEPFAR's targeted use of AIDS money to marginalize minorities, undermine access to condoms and reproductive choice, foster stigma, and deny people access to life-saving medicines and treatment support. Meanwhile, she's busy with her accountability for the US military budget.

Rice's strategic, rhetorical posture of respect for identity and difference contrast starkly with her actions as a policy maker and politician, and raise the alarm on the threat posed by the Bush administration. International feminism's core moral insight—that women are due the same rights and dignity as men—has been co-opted as a Trojan horse for imperial wars fought in the name of free-market capitalist democracy: When we talk about respect for women, we are referring to a moral truth. Women are free by nature, equal in dignity and entitled the same rights, the same protections, and the same opportunities as men. This is a standard that, quite frankly, we in the United States have fallen short of in our history. It took our country 130 years before we interpreted the phrase "all men are created equal" flexibly enough to let ladies vote. Whether it is assistance to women in Darfur or the fight against human trafficking, the United States champions respect for women because it is morally right. But we also recognize that respect for women is a prerequisite for success of countries in the modern world. In the dynamic 21st century no society can expect to flourish with half its people sitting on the sidelines, with no opportunity to develop their talents, to contribute to their economy, or to play an equal part in the lives of their nations. Last year a group of Kuwaiti suffragists sent me a T-shirt and it makes that point very well. It says, "Half a democracy is not a democracy." That was the slogan that the women of Kuwait used to demand and to win their right to vote.

Rice made no reference in the speech she gave in 2006 to the fact that America continues to do business with Saudi Arabia, nor to the global environmental crisis fostered by the Bush administration's anti-green policies.[5] These economic and environmental realities, it seems, have no bearing on democracy or women's rights. Refreshing though it may be to find Aretha Franklin's anthem on Rice's list of favorite pieces of music, and thus as a potential reference point for her international foreign policy, "Respect" is a gloriously ambivalent term when applied to women who, the world over, are subordinated and constrained to obey fathers, husbands, boyfriends, and patriarchal authority, and are commonly subjected to denigration, rape, torture, and abuse by religious fundamentalisms and states fostered and economically bolstered by oil-hungry American capital.[6]

By claiming the export of respect and, more specifically, democratic enfranchisement for women as constitutive elements of explicitly anti-Islamic US foreign policy, Rice gives voice to policy that, contrary to all historical and political accuracy, proposes feminism as inherently Western, an intrinsic feature of capitalist liberal democracy, and as profoundly anti-Islamic. This cultural relativism is now familiar in conversations about women's rights in different parts of the world. Moreover, the manner in which the secretary of state makes high-profile statements about how America is doing its bit for Muslim sisters is to fail quite spectacularly to acknowledge that anti-Western sentiment throughout many parts of the Muslim world means that "indigenous" feminist movements are likely to be politically damaged if seen as being supported, or in Rice's version of current US foreign policy, instigated, by the West.

In the hands of the evangelical right, the once universalist moral claims to equal dignity and individual freedom in the fight against racial and sexual oppression are being wielded as a weapon of civilization against barbarism, and the mark of cultural progress:

> In Afghanistan, I met the young players of a girls' soccer team. It was quite a striking contrast from the Afghanistan in which, just four years ago, the Taliban turned soccer stadiums given to them by the international community into killing fields and condemned women to death for learning to read.

When they want to suppress people, they always go after the right to read. Slaves were not allowed to read, because if you can read, you may begin to redefine what your horizons are. And so that women in Afghanistan are now being taught to read openly and supported by their government is an amazing fact and shows that Afghanistan is progressing.[7]

These would indeed be amazing facts if they were true. The plight of women in Afghanistan remains appalling. Against all reality and evidence, Rice is claiming a victory that has not in fact been won. Amnesty International's 2005 report, "Afghanistan: Women still under attack—a systematic failure to protect,"[8] documents in detail the continuing failures of both the Afghan government and international governments and agencies in taking sufficient steps to effect real change to eliminate the continuing vicious cycle of violence and discrimination against women and their rights in all aspects of their lives. Moreover, presenting feminism, like democracy, as an American export, and thus inherently Western, is a sure way to damage and undermine indigenous feminist and women's rights movements.

Identity and difference are valuable analytical and interpretive tools for understanding the repression and denial that lurk behind the structural inequalities and asymmetries of racialized, sexualized, and gendered power. However, both Rice's public political policies and personal strategies for self-fashioning provide an urgent reminder that racially and sexually marked identities are the manifestation of inequality and injustice, not their cause. A distorted politics of identity is ideologically central to the neoconservative worldview. According to this logic, if one is Muslim, one is a threat and, therefore, a legitimate target. Further, Rice would have the world believe that everything that happens in a Muslim-majority country happens in the name of Islam. Identity can be used as both a tool of fragmentation and oppression, and a tool of common cause and liberation. But as Condoleezza Rice demonstrates, in the current global climate, we focus on identity at the expense of politics at our peril.

Notes

1. Antonia Felix, *The Condoleezza Rice Story,* London: Methuen, 2005, p.113.

2. Acceptance speech, Woman of Valor Award, Independent Women's Forum in May 2006, http://www.state.gov/secretary/rm/2006/66139.htm.

3. Kenyon Farrow, "Open letter to Secretary of State Condoleezza Rice," January 10, 2006, http://www.towardfreedom.com/home/content/view/722/.

4. Michel Muller, interview with Angela Davis, *l'Humanité,* December 12, 2005, see http://www.humaniteinenglish.com/article.php3?id_article=15.

5. Acceptance speech, Woman of Valor Award, Independent Women's Forum in May 2006, http://www.state.gov/secretary/rm/2006/66139.htm.

6. The famously euphonious Rice recently selected Aretha Franklin's "Respect" as one of the ten best musical works in her list for a recent newspaper article. See http://enjoyment.independent.co.uk/music/features/article484642.ece.

7. Acceptance speech, Woman of Valor Award, Independent Women's Forum in May 2006, http://www.state.gov/secretary/rm/2006/66139.htm.

8. For full report, see http://web.amnesty.org/library/index/engasa110072005.

BEHIND THE MASK

Haifa Zangana

The actors in Greek tragedy were hired and paid by the state. By the middle of the fifth century three actors were required for the performance of a tragedy. Since most plays have more than two or three characters, all three actors played multiple roles. Since women were not allowed to take part in dramatic productions, male actors had to play female roles. The playing of multiple roles, both male and female, was made possible by the use of masks, which prevented the audience from identifying the face of any actor with one specific character in the play and helped eliminate the physical incongruity of men impersonating women.[1]

Two women have held the position of US secretary of state in the last decade.

     Under President Clinton, Madeleine Albright was the first female secretary of state, and the highest-ranking woman in the history of the US government. Condoleezza Rice was the first female US national security advisor. Under President Bush, she is the second woman to be appointed secretary of state. Both women are highly educated and renowned for their intellect. Are their life experiences, their gender, and in Rice's case, her race, somehow reflected in their policies as secretary of state? Let's consider the fate of the Iraqi people, and of the women there in particular.

In 1991, in the aftermath of 45 days of bombardment by US warplanes, the Iraqi people discovered they were to be subject to "one of the most comprehensive campaigns of economic sanctions in modern history."[2] Twelve years of severe deprivation followed the brutal attacks by shells tipped with depleted uranium.

"Even the most basic things like ear-drops and antibiotics are in desperately short supply," an Iraqi doctor said. One Iraqi exile tried to find people who were prepared to smuggle eye drops to his 80-year-old mother in Baghdad. "She is badly in need of an operation," he said, "but they are so short of anesthetics that only emergencies are being carried out."[3]

On December 6, 1995, I sent a small padded envelope to my nieces and nephews in Mosul, north of Iraq. It contained one pencil case, three erasers, three sharpeners, six fountain pens, two markers, one glue stick and two ballpoint pens. It was marked "gift for children." Several weeks later the envelope was returned to me, stamped: "Due to international sanctions against Iraq, we are not able to forward your packet."[4]

In May 1996, the "60 Minutes" correspondent Lesley Stahl asked Madeline Albright, then US Ambassador to the UN: "We have heard that half a million children have died [as a result of sanctions against Iraq]. I mean, that is more children than died in Hiroshima. And, you know, is the price worth it?"

Albright responded: "I think that is a very hard choice, but the price, we think, the price is worth it."

On November 16, 2004, when President Bush announced he had nominated Condoleezza Rice, his national security advisor and one of his closest counselors, to replace Colin Powell as secretary of state, he made this statement: "The secretary of state is America's face to the world, and in Rice the world will see the strength, grace and decency of our country."

Is this what Iraqis see?

Rice has loyally served the Bush administration in its military campaigns in Afghanistan and Iraq, including in the handling of fraudulent intelligence before the September 11, 2001 attacks. She has contributed to the planning of the preemptive war on Iraq and the subsequent catastrophic occupation of the country.

"I believe strongly it was the right strategic decision," Rice said.

"I know we've made tactical errors, thousands of them, I'm sure," she said in a speech at Blackburn's Chatham House, a center for independent research on global issues.[5]

Mistakes? Tactical errors? Let's look at a few: the lies over weapons of mass destruction originally used to justify the war; arbitrary arrests; the torture of prisoners and the round-up of more than 30,000 detainees, including women and children, in Abu Ghraib and other US/UK-controlled prisons and camps; the siege and bombardment of cities; the use of depleted uranium and white phosphorus; and the destruction of mosques, schools, and private residences. Corruption has been transferred from Mr. Hussein's elites to another set of unaccountable oligarchs. As of May, 2006, three years after the occupation, Iraq's poorer households are still worried about food, one out of every three children is malnourished, and nine percent of Iraqi children are acutely malnourished. 25 percent of students under the age of 15 have dropped out of school.[6]

Is the killing of over 150,000 civilians a mistake? When is a mistake a war crime?

Most killings of Iraqis go unreported. With no names, faces, or identities, the victims of the American invasion cease to be registered as human beings. They are "the enemy," "collateral damage," or statistics to argue about. Now they are counted by Rice as "mistakes," or "tactical errors."

A'beer Qassim al-Janaby is one of them: a 15-year-old Iraqi girl who was with her family in Mahmudiyah, 20 miles south of Baghdad, when US troops raided their house. A group of American soldiers have been charged with her rape and the murder of her father, mother, and nine-year-old sister. They are also accused of setting A'beer's body on fire. The al-Janaby family lived near a US checkpoint. As usual, a US spokesman described the killings as a response to "Sunni Arab insurgents active in the area," contrary to local eyewitnesses.

Unlike A'beer, Eman Waleed, a nine-year-old child, has survived Haditha's massacre, the My Lai of the Iraq war, to tell the tale about Haditha, a town in western Iraq, where US Marines are suspected of having killed "up to 24 Iraqi civilians in November 2005 and covering up the deaths. Among these were two women and a child, who died after a building collapsed under heavy fire and crushed them." [7]

Eman, who witnessed the horrific killing of her family by US marines on November 19, 2005, described them entering their house: "First, they went into my father's room, where he was reading the Koran. We heard shots." According to Eman, the Marines then entered the living room. "I couldn't see their faces very well—only their guns sticking into the doorway. I watched them shoot my grandfather, first in the chest and then in the head. Then they killed my granny." She said the troops started firing toward the corner of the room where she and her eight-year-old brother Abdul Rahman, were hiding; the other adults shielded the children from the bullets but died in the process. Eman says her leg was hit by a piece of metal and Abdul Rahman was shot near his shoulder. "We were lying there, bleeding, and it hurt so much. Afterward, some Iraqi soldiers came. They carried us in their arms. I was crying, shouting, 'Why did you do this to our family?' And one Iraqi soldier tells me, 'We didn't do it. The Americans did.'" [8]

"In February an infantry colonel went to Haditha for a weeklong probe in which he interviewed marines, survivors and doctors at the morgue, according to military officials close to the investigation. The probe concluded that the civilians were in fact killed by marines and not by an insurgent's bomb and that no insurgents appeared to be in the first two houses raided by the marines. The probe found, however, that the deaths were the result of collateral damage rather than malicious intent." [9]

In its human rights report for the months of July and August 2006, the U.N. Assistance Mission for Iraq (UNAMI) affirms that the number of civilians killed violently in the country was an unprecedented 3,590 in July and 3,009 in August. [10] Killings, kidnappings, and torture continue to occur at an alarming daily rate. Professionals from the judiciary, health, and education faculties are particularly targeted in the violence.[11]

One of the long-term damaging effects engulfing Iraq under occupation is the systematic assassination of the country's academics. "Even according to conservative estimates, over 250 educators have been assassinated, and many hundreds more have disappeared. With thousands fleeing the country in fear for their lives, not only is Iraq undergoing a major brain drain, the secular middle class, which has refused to be co-opted by the US occupation, is being decimated, with far-reaching consequences for the future of Iraq."[12]

On July 14, 2004, veteran correspondent Robert Fisk reported from Iraq that "University staff suspect that there is a campaign to strip Iraq of its academics, to complete the destruction of Iraq's cultural identity which began when the American army entered Baghdad."

Isam al-Rawi, a geologist at Baghdad University and head of the Association of University Lecturers, records the dead. He says that about 300 academics and university administrators have been assassinated in a mysterious wave of murders since the American occupation of Iraq began in 2003. About 2,000 others, he says, have fled the country.[13]

One of those killed in March 2006 was Kays Juma, another professor at the University of Baghdad, where he taught agriculture to graduate students. His assassination by a private security guard was reported by Western media because he had an Australian passport. The Associated Press reported:

> Paul Jordan of AKE Asia Pacific, an Australian security consulting company, which has had contractors in Iraq since the war began, told ABC radio he was not surprised by the incident. "This is something that happens every day in Iraq," he said. "The American troops and other troops over there and security companies are shooting innocent people that do get too close to convoys or who do the wrong thing in traffic or just happen to be in the wrong place at the wrong time and look suspicious.

On January 28, 2006, Abdul Razaq al-Na'as, a Baghdad university professor in his fifties, drove from his office at Baghdad University. Two cars blocked his, and gunmen opened fire, killing him instantly.

Baghdad universities alone have mourned the killing of over 80 members of staff. The minister of education stated recently that during 2005, 296 members of education staff were killed and 133 wounded.[14] Not one of these crimes has been investigated by the occupation forces or the Iraqi puppet governments.

The Director-General of UNESCO, Koïchiro Matsuura, in April 2006, appealed on the international community to support Iraqi academics and intellectuals and called for measures to protect them from "A heinous campaign of violence."[15]

Rice, a former academic, continues to wear her mask.

According to a recent Human Rights Watch report: "The military and the Bush Administration appear to be in denial. Both have consistently portrayed abuse cases from Iraq as exceptional and perpetrators as lone and independent actors—'rotten apples'—despite evidence that military intelligence officers and higher-echelon military and civilian leaders knew about or may even have authorized abusive techniques that were used against detainees. Such sweeping denials, and the military's general failure to place any blame on leadership for abuses that occurred, have hindered candid assessments about the detainee abuse problem."[16]

"When Rice was growing up, her father stood guard at the entrance of her neighborhood with a rifle to keep the Klan's nightriders away."[17] If gun registration had been mandatory, her father's weapons would have been confiscated, leaving them defenseless against the Ku Klux Klan.[18]

It is ironic that fathers in "liberated Iraq" now stand guard in their neighborhoods with rifles to keep the nightriders sanctioned by Bush and Rice away.

A'beer's rape and murder is neither incidental nor the product of a US soldier's "personality disorder": it is part of the pattern of racist "mistakes" and "tactical errors" that include Abu Ghraib, and the Haditha and Ishaqi massacres.

There will be no end to the mayhem in Iraq as long as Iraq remains occupied by forces that enjoy immunity from prosecution under Iraqi law and as long as the occupation authorities continue to treat Iraqi citizens with racist contempt in order to justify plundering the nation's wealth and depriving its people of their most fundamental rights under international law and human rights conventions.

What started as war on terror in one country has developed into many brutal wars for world domination by the US. The race and gender of the occupiers, and how they use issues of race and gender in their propaganda, is irrelevant for occupied people. For Iraqis, as well as for Palestinians, Lebanese, and Afghans, occupation has is inherently racist, a legacy Condoleezza Rice and Madeleine Albright have to live with.

Notes

1. http://depthome.brooklyn.cuny.edu/classics/dunkle/studyguide/tragedy.htm.
2. http://www.commondreams.org/views04/1201-24.htm.
3. *BMJ* 1994;309:898 (8 October http://bmj.bmjjournals.com/cgi/content/full/309/6959/898.
4. http://politics.guardian.co.uk/comment/story/0,9115,793492,00.html.
5. http://www.cnn.com/2006/WORLD/europe/03/31/rice.straw.liverpool/index.html.
6. Food Insecurity in Iraq Persists: Children Suffer. http://www.unicef.org/media/media_33915.html.
7. http://news.bbc.co.uk/1/hi/world/middle_east/5039420.stm.
8. http://www.time.com/time/world/printout/0,8816,1174649,00.html.
9. *Ibid.*
10. http://www.reliefweb.int/library/documents/2006/unami-irq-31aug.pdf.
11. http://www.isria.com/FILES/2006/JULY/072006_01037.htm.
12. Dr. Isam Al Rawi, see http://www.ceri-sciences-po.org/cerifr/cherlist/lafourcade.htm.
13. http://www.usatoday.com/news/world/iraq/2005-01-16-academics-assassinations_x.htm.
14. http://education.guardian.co.uk/higher/comment/story/0,,1719508,00.html.
15. http://portal.unesco.org/es/ev.php-.URL_ID=33249&URL_DO=DO_TOPIC&URL_SECTION=201.html.
16. http://hrw.org/reports/2006/us0706/1.htm#_Toc141074582.
17. http://www.washingtonpost.com/wp-dyn/content/article/2005/10/24/AR2005102401370.html.
18. B. Denise Hawkins, "Condoleezza Rice's Secret Weapon," *Christianity Today*, September/October 2002.

BIG LOVE

Ann E. Butler

Condi

Named after the Italian music-related expression *con dolcezza*, meaning "with sweetness," Condoleezza Rice was born on November 14, 1954 in Birmingham, Alabama, six months after Brown vs. Board of Education, the US Supreme Court decision which dismantled the legal basis for racial segregation in schools and other public facilities, but not in other areas of American social and cultural life. Rice was raised in the Titusville neighborhood, a black middle-class enclave in Birmingham.

Rice is the product of a family committed to the notion of formal education as a means of advancement and personal achievement. She is the granddaughter of a religiously devout sharecropper who became a Presbyterian minister to fund his formal education. She is the daughter of John and Angelena Rice, hard-working educators who instilled in her the belief that education and achievement were the best defense against prejudice. Both parents were equally religious, her mother a music teacher and church organist, and her father a second-generation minister at Westminster Presbyterian Church. During her childhood, Rice's parents actively played down the stinging reality of Jim Crow racism and segregation. Rice was encouraged to use facilities at home rather than segregated washrooms and water fountains. When asked about her childhood, Rice reminisces about piano lessons and brief attempts at ballet, not the loss of her childhood friend Denise McNair, one of the four little girls killed in the racially motivated 1963 bombing of the Sixteenth Street Baptist Church.

Comfortable only with factual statements as a means of minimizing the emotional impact of growing up in a racist environment, when asked about the personal impact of segregation, Rice acknowledges that racism was a reality, "The fact that our society is not colorblind is a statement of fact."[1] In published interviews, Rice has said that, "despite growing up with racial segregation, personal expectations were high.... My parents had me absolutely convinced that, well, you may not be able to have a hamburger at Woolworth's but you can be president of the United States."[2] In an interview with Eugene Robinson of the *Washington Post*, she said, "I've always said about Birmingham that because race was everything, race was nothing."[3]

Initially trained as a concert pianist, Rice graduated from the University of Denver in 1974 at the astonishing age of 19 with a degree in political science. One year later, in 1975, she earned a master's degree from the University of Notre Dame. By her early twenties, in 1981, she could speak four languages and she had earned her Ph.D. in international affairs from the Graduate School of International Studies at the University of Denver. By her mid-thirties, Rice had gone farther in academia and government than any of her peers in international relations. Her impressive professional achievements include:

> First black female awarded a fellowship to the International Security and Arms Control Center at Stanford University in 1981.

> Hoover Institution National Fellow from 1985 to 1986.

> Hoover Institute Senior Fellow from 1991-1993.

First black female provost at Stanford University from
1993 to 1999.

Served on the Board of Directors for the Chevron
Corporation, the Charles Schwab Corporation, Trans-
america Corporation, Hewlett Packard, and the Boards
of several philanthropic organizations and conservative
think tanks.

First black female appointed US national security
advisor from 2000 to 2004.

First black female appointed US secretary of state from
2005 to the present.

Rice has been fortunate to have had several mentors in her life,
most of whom are extremely prominent in political and academic
circles. Many influential white men have played a significant role
in creating major opportunities for advancement for Rice. Josef
Korbel, a Czech refugee, scholar, and professor of international
relations at the University of Denver, encouraged Rice to pursue
a career in international relations. (Korbel is also the father of
Madeleine Albright, the former secretary of state in the Clinton
Administration.) Gerhard Casper, president of Stanford University from 1991 to 2000, named Rice provost of Stanford in 1993,
when she was only 38 years old, although she had no administrative experience in higher education. Brent Scowcroft, national
security advisor to Presidents Ford and George H. W. Bush, and
a close friend of the Bush family, appointed Rice to the National
Security Council in 1989, as chief authority on the Soviet Union.
Scowcroft also introduced Rice to George H. W. Bush and the
Bush family. George P. Shultz, former secretary of state during
the Reagan and Bush administrations, introduced Rice to experts from the Hoover Institution at Stanford, a right-wing think
tank. Rice served as head of George H. W. Bush's foreign policy
advisors, dubbed the Vulcans, during his presidential campaign.

Bush also introduced Rice to his son, W. At his father's suggestion, W. named Rice as his foreign policy advisor and mentor and was also part of his Presidential campaign's response team. W. named Rice as his national security advisor during his first term and as the country's secretary of state during his second term in office.

Rice is said to have changed her political affiliation from Democratic to Republican in 1982, although she informally advised the Gary Hart presidential campaign in 1984. In 1988, she was offered a position on Michael Dukakis's presidential campaign by Madeline Albright but declined, claiming she was a Republican. By 1991, friends noticed that she had become more staunchly conservative and more identified with the Republican Party. [4]

In 1993, a Chevron oil tanker was named after Rice. The ship was christened at a ceremony in Rio de Janeiro. A few years later the name of the tanker was changed to the Altair Voyager so as to not draw further attention to more relationships between members of the Bush Administration and the oil industry.

Rice reflects the aspirations of Americans who believe in the power of sheer individualism and singular achievement, not collective identity. One of the guiding principles promoted within minority communities in the US is that as you succeed in climbing, you are obliged to reach back and assist others in joining you. Surrounded for most of her professional life with a number of immensely influential white men who have served as mentors, Rice in no way appears to embody shared principles of collective identity. Rice considers herself a Black patrician,[5] and someone who "believes so firmly that the individual (or at least, the extraordinary individual, like herself) can triumph over imposed limitations that she is almost insulted by the idea that collective action and government intervention were essential to her own life."[6] Ironically, during the period of Rice's formal education she was in many ways the classic beneficiary of affirmative action, a viewpoint she would vehemently deny.

Impeccably organized, gracious and poised, Rice is a shrewd tactical logician, with a fiercely acquisitive mind. She is the ultimate performer who can master any level of detail and reduce it to perfectly articulated packages of certainty and conviction. She is uncomfortable openly acknowledging the complexity of a situation, as if expressions of ambiguity represented a lessening of her performance of absolute assurance, discipline, and control.

Rice is a paradoxical woman. From a young age, she knew that she had to be twice as good as whites in order to gain an equal footing. She is a politically astute performer with a brilliant mind and a keen sense of diplomacy, which has helped her maneuver into the heart of one of conservative America's most powerful families, the Bushes.

In Washington, nothing matters more than access to and face time with the President. What distinguishes Rice from her predecessors is her personal and professional closeness to George W. Bush. In a *New Yorker* profile, Nicholas Lemann notes that, "It isn't just that she briefs him every morning, attends several formal meetings with him every week, and sees or speaks to him several times in the course of a typical day; it's also that she spends many weekends as the Bushes' guest at Camp David or at the Presidential ranch in Crawford, Texas."[7]

What is the basis of the relationship? Rice is also referred to as Bush's work-wife.[8] For someone who rarely falters when speaking publicly, Rice made a revealing verbal slip when referring to W. at a 2004 dinner party hosted by *New York Times* D.C. bureau chief Philip Taubman and his wife Felicity Barringer. Rice was overheard saying, "'As I was telling my husb-' and then stopping herself abruptly, before saying, 'As I was telling President Bush.'"[9]

Just as Rice has surrounded herself professionally with influential white men, Bush surrounds himself with ambitious and charismatic women. Lemann notes that the common ground between Bush and Rice encompasses the following: "religious faith and football fandom and a sardonic sense of humor; more broadly, an outside-inside-the-establishment feeling and a tendency to see life in terms of good guys and bad guys; even more broadly, a complete absence of self-doubt, . . . Rice and Bush seem to reinforce, rather than challenge or balance, each other."[10] W. and Rice's religious convictions not only inform their personal relationship but also affect their worldview. In another *New Yorker* article, "What turned Brent Scowcroft against the Bush Administration," Jeffrey Goldberg notes the growing rift between Scowcroft and his protégé, in terms of Rice's shift from a pragmatic and realist sociopolitical worldview to a moralistic and evangelical outlook. "Rice's conversion to the world view of George W. Bush is still a mystery, however. Privately, many of her ex-colleagues from the first President Bush's National Security Council say that it is rooted in her Christian faith, which leads her to see the world in moralistic terms, much as the President does."[11]

Laura

Laura Bush has lived a very circumscribed, simple life since she was born in Midland, Texas on November 4, 1946 to Harold and Jenna Welch. Laura claims she was inspired by her second grade teacher to become a public school teacher. In 1968 she earned a bachelor of science degree in education from Southern Methodist University in Texas. She taught for a few years in the Dallas and Houston public school systems. In 1973 she earned a master of library science degree from the University of Texas at Austin and worked as a public school librarian in the Austin public school system. In 1977, she met and married George W. Bush. Once married, she gave up her career. Aside from her years in Washington, DC as First Lady, Laura Bush has spent all of her adult life living in Texas.

Often characterized as a nonthreatening and traditional woman, during the 2000 Presidential campaign, the only dirt journalists could dig up about Laura was the story of a car accident she had as a teen. In 1963, at the age of 17, while driving a Chevrolet sedan, Laura ran through a stop sign in Midland, Texas. She drove through an intersection and struck a Corvair driven by 17-year-old Michael Douglas, Laura's boyfriend at the time, killing him. Laura and her passenger were taken to a local hospital and treated for minor injuries. No charges were ever filed.

Emblematic of the compliant and selfless female caretaker, Laura

Bush has played it safe for all of her life. Laura's White House Webpage describes her in the following way: First a wife, and then a mother, then a college graduate, and finally, a woman with a professional career as a public school teacher and public school librarian. When Laura's White House handlers want to promote her as a professional woman they emphasize her career as a children's librarian. Not just any type of librarian or information specialist, but a children's public school librarian, or kiddie lit librarian, rather like a Mr. Rogers of the library world.

Librarianship as a profession is founded on the democratic principles of access to information and intellectual freedom, principles Laura's husband's administration has actively suppressed in large part through the Patriot Act and also through massive cuts in public-service spending. Rather than highlight these democratic ideals of librarianship in their portrayal of Laura, because they conflict with their politically conservative policies, the White House instead chooses to emphasize the stereotype of the kiddie lit librarian as a docile, obedient and unthreatening professional and reap political capital from the fact that Laura was once a public school librarian. Laura's White House Webpage takes the kiddie lit stereotype to the hilt. The site includes Laura's recommended reading list which includes only the safest children's books. Selected titles are listed in sappy categories such as: "Family Reading," "Books to read to and with Young Children," and "Special Comfort Books." The list represents the predictable canon of kiddie lit: *Goodnight Moon*, *Mother Goose Rhymes*, *Little Women*, and *Little House on the Prairie*. Progressive classics such as *Paper Bag Princess*, *Heather has Two Mommies*, and *William's Doll* are nowhere to be found.

Who is Laura Bush? We know she's elusive and a masterful deflector. Publicly she's been referred to as a Stepford Wife, the woman with the Xanax demeanor; the Bush Administration's fabric softener; and by her husband as the "lump in the bed."[12] As First Lady, Laura's role in the Bush administration is to "lull."[13] She's called upon to diminish controversy, to soft peddle her husband's ultraconservative policies, and to reinforce the compassion in the "compassionate conservative" platform her husband ran on.

When asked for her opinion on a political issue, she gives a non-committal reply. When Laura is portrayed as an advocate, we hear about non-controversial, non-partisan issues like early childhood education, child literacy and reading, and the rights of women in Afghanistan and Iraq. Often thought to be more liberal than her husband, when asked for her opinion on the reproductive rights of women in the US, Laura gives noncommittal reply and says that all opinions are important.

How does Laura measure up as a librarian? If she was serious about supporting the principles and ideals of librarianship, she would actively voice her opposition to the Patriot Act and other forms of censorship. She would also work to keep public libraries from closing due to continuing local, state, and federal budget cuts. Giving money to public libraries through her Laura Bush Foundation is great, but shortsighted when libraries can't afford staff and infrastructure expenses. Ultimately Laura should work against legitimizing the traditional stereotype of librarians as quiet, benign, and obedient.

Condi and Laura

Condi and Laura share some key common traits and characteristics: they're both women; they're both immensely loyal to W. A symptom of that devotion is their consistent deference to him. They never publicly contradict him. They're both silent arbiters who play powerful hidden roles and rarely make their personal views publicly known.

Differences between Condi and Laura are more significant and telling, and these striking differences ultimately benefit W. Condi is hawkish; she's often asked to play the bad cop. Laura is a sentimental apologist who is often relied upon to play the good cop. Condi is an absolutist, which is clearly evident in current US foreign policy. Laura on the other hand reflects compromise in most aspects of her life. Condi's life history is complex and paradoxical; Laura's is circumscribed and predictable. Condi is ambitious; Laura is complacent. Laura is married, Condi is single. Condi is W.'s work wife, Laura is his real wife.

Through marital, personal, and professional ties and affiliations, W. is the principal recipient and beneficiary of all the qualities and characteristics listed above. Condi and Laura make W. look good. The sizeable differences between them serve to more fully substantiate and supplement W. giving him the appearance of a wealth of qualities and characteristics that he sorely lacks.

Currently, both Condi and Laura share uniquely high approval ratings with the American public. A January 2006 CNN/ *USA Today/* Gallup poll gave Laura an 82 percent approval rating, among the highest ratings Gallup has ever recorded for a first lady.[14] With the approval ratings of most of the White House administration plummeting, Condi's approval ratings are actually on the rise.

As of April 2006, W.'s approval ratings were at an all-time low. As his ratings plummet further, he relies all the more on Laura and Condi to redeem his popularity. With midterm elections approaching, W.'s low popularity lacks appeal for any GOP campaigning. Laura is picking up the slack, filling a vacuum, and becoming a strong political money machine. She's raising funds for GOP candidates by campaigning in districts where her husband would be considered political poison.

Why are Laura and Condi considered more appealing to the American public right now? Laura is clearly a palliative. Her ratings are so high, in part because W.'s are so low. The American public's approval and endorsement of Laura is symptomatic of the public's disapproval of Bush. Where he represents a deficit, she represents a clear political surplus.

The Perfect Threesome

Sandwiched between his work wife and his real wife, W., has always relied upon an association and affiliation with talented and loyal women to supplement who he is and what he represents. Karen Hughes and Harriet Miers certainly also belong in this league. As Maureen Dowd recently put it in a *New York Times* editorial, "All the President's Women," "W. loves being surrounded by tough women who steadfastly devote their entire lives to doting on him, like the vestal virgins guarding the sacred fire, serving as custodians for his values and watchdogs for his reputation."[15] This "union of the three," Condi, Laura, and W., represents the Republican party's response to affirmative action and feminism.

What dynamics are put into play with the packaging of these three? Condi provides intellectual substance, articulation, and political legitimacy with new constituencies. Laura provides compassionate cover for W., emphasizing intimate selling points to female audiences. W. provides access to a world stage for Condi and Laura.

The Bush team has cynically and subversively altered the image of the conservative party. They've strategically given the party of tired, old, white men a female facelift, made it appear more inclusive, and further eroded the traditional advantage held by the Democratic party with women and Blacks. One of the key strategies in their arsenal is wife deployment: work wife and real wife.

Notes

1. Eugene Robinson, "What Rice Can't See," *Washington Post*, October 25, 2005, p. A21.

2. Profile: Condoleezza Rice, *BBC News Profile*, March 30, 2006.

3. Eugene Robinson, "What Rice Can't See," *Washington Post*, October 25, 2005, p. A21.

4. Nicholas Lemann, "Without a Doubt: Has Condoleezza Rice changed George W. Bush, or has he changed her?," *New Yorker*, October 14, 2002, p. 177.

5. *Ibid.*, p. 168.

6. *Ibid.*, p. 169.

7. *Ibid.*, p. 166.

8. Timothy Noah, "Prexy Sks Wrk Wf: Condoleezza Rice's Promotion Creates a Void," *Slate Magazine*, November 17, 2004.

10. Debora Schoenemann with Spencer Morgan, "Armani's Exchange—Condi's Slip...Forget the Alamo," *New York Magazine*, April 26, 2004.
Nicholas Lemann, "Without a Doubt: Has Condoleezza Rice changed George W. Bush, or has he changed her?," *New Yorker*, October 14, 2002, p. 177.

11. Jeffrey Goldberg, "Breaking Ranks: What turned Brent Scowcroft against the Bush Administration?," *New Yorker*, October 31, 2005, p. 60.

12. Associated Press, "Bush, The Record Fund-Raiser," *CBS News online*, July 5, 2003.

13. See Laura Flanders, *Bushwomen: Tales of a Cynical Species*, Verso, 2004.

14. William Douglas, "With President sliding in the polls, Laura Bush picks up the slack," *Knight Ridder Newspapers*, April 25, 2005.

15. Maureen Dowd, "All the President's Women," *New York Times*, October 5, 2005, p. 27.

CONDOLEEZZA RICE IS SPECIAL

Astra Taylor

Twice ranked as *Forbes Magazine*'s "most powerful woman in the world," there is no doubt Condoleezza Rice's actions impact the lives of Americans and people around the globe. Yet national interest in her goes well beyond issues of policy and tends to focus on her personal life, an inclination that often obscures meaningful discussion of her role in the Bush administration.

Newspapers regularly print glowing profiles of Rice, commenting on her childhood in Birmingham, Alabama, her fitness regime, her apartment's décor, her amateur chamber music playing, all without making mention of her lies to the 9/11 Commission, her exploitation of American fears about Iraq's chimerical weapons of mass destruction, or her defense of the federal government's inaction after Hurricane Katrina. For example, of the nearly three thousand *New York Times* articles that came up when I searched the paper's online archive, only six made any mention of Rice's theory of "transformational diplomacy," a key component of President Bush's 2006 national security strategy. The secretary has described this "bold" new approach as one that "not only reports about the world as it is, but seeks to change the world itself;" in other words, it's a form of diplomacy that does not deal with countries as they are, but proactively seeks to manipulate their politics.[1]

While *The Guardian* covers this news like an earthquake in the diplomatic world, calling "transformational diplomacy" a "dramatic change in US diplomacy,"[2] the *New York Times* is too busy reporting rumors. A September, 13, 2006 article, inspired by speculation about Rice's relationship to Peter MacKay, Canada's handsome foreign minister, is a case in point. "The single, sophisticated American Secretary of State once drew notice for wearing black stiletto knee-high boots with an above-the-knee black skirt while reviewing American troops in Germany, so she is bound to attract gossip," reads the 1,000-word treatise—complete with two color photographs—on Rice's possible flirtation, before coming forth with a disclaimer. "There is no evidence whatsoever to suggest that Ms. Rice and Mr. MacKay are linked by anything more than their shared status as singletons."[3]

Which begs the simple question: Why bother writing about a nonexistent affair? What is it about Condoleezza Rice that makes even the unfounded fascinating? Dick Cheney, for example, will never be the subject of so much interest and conjecture, largely because there's nothing particularly provocative about the Vice President: a Yale University dropout, a former CEO of Halliburton, a multimillionaire oilman. In other words, a quintessential white male member of the ruling class with no mystery, no improbable trajectory. Rice, in contrast, transcends stereotypes and expectations.

Ultimately, the fascination with Rice tells us more about our culture's assumptions and expectations than it does about her. It speaks more about rather recently enshrined, though still hotly contested, ideas about race, class, and gender than it does about one highly intelligent ultra-ambitious individual who also happens to be African-American and female.

No doubt, it's precisely these expectations and assumptions that make Rice such a highly effective political operative, causing some feminists to commend the Bush administration for her appointment on the basis of chromosomes alone and to compel the president of the National Association for the Advancement of Colored People (NAACP) to come repeatedly to her defense.

According to national surveys, Rice consistently ranks in polls as one of the nation's best-liked leaders. "The striking thing on the Republican side is Rice's continued popularity," said Carroll Doherty of the Pew Research Center. "We found that she had significant crossover appeal to independents and even to some Democrats."[4] Ergo, Barack Obama, who won his seat as the only African-American currently serving in the Senate as an antiwar candidate, voted to confirm Rice as Secretary of State.

In other words, despite the fact Rice has been instrumental in making a farce of international diplomacy around Iraq and, by doing so, paved the way for an illegal war based on purposeful lies she helped propagate, people continue to be sympathetic to her, including a good number of liberals. I would wager that many of these individuals believe, somehow, that Rice's skin color and gender make her more sensible, more humane, more venerable than her warmongering profit-mad colleagues—ideas reinforced by the barrage of human interest pieces printed about her. At the same time, the inverse is also true: Some react by hating her all the more, castigating her as a traitor. This logic says it is worse for Rice to be a right-wing extremist than the white men she works with. Because of her race and gender, she should be more aligned with the disenfranchised, sensitive to other people of color, attuned to sisterhood. Both perspectives point to the roots of Rice's remarkable status in our collective consciousness, and both reaffirm the myth of Rice's exceptionalism.

To make sense of this situation we have to go back to the early days of the civil rights movement, the first signs of feminism, and the rise of identity politics (the movements for self-determination that evolved out of the tumult of the 1960s and 70s, such as Black Nationalism, the American Indian Movement, Women's Liberation, and the struggle for gay, transgender, and disability rights). Since the apex of the Civil Rights Movements, related battles continue to be fought on college campuses, with students and faculty advocating for ethnic and women's studies departments and more inclusive curricula, and on the national stage in debates about the Equal Rights Amendment (ERA) and the Americans with Disabilities Act (ADA), and through controversial issues like school busing, affirmative action, and abortion. Over the years many of the principles driving these struggles—diversity, inclusiveness, multiculturalism, equal opportunity—have seeped into public consciousness, seemingly for the better. Rice's success owes a huge debt to these developments, and one she refuses to acknowledge.

Conservatives initially responded to these hard-won progressive gains by mounting a counterattack. Through the 80s and 90s, pundits sounded the alarm about left-wing "thought police" and "feminazis" on college campuses. Blue-collar workers were told blacks and women were taking their jobs. Religious leaders claimed the traditional family was under siege by homosexuals and ambitious career women. Sensitivity to matters of gender, race and class was belittled as "political correctness" and the demands of disadvantaged minorities were dismissed as the incessant whining of "special-interest groups." The resulting "culture war" raged for years, and the right was successful in rolling back the liberal advance and strengthening its grip on the American imagination.

And yet, in recent years, conservatives have changed their tack. They have adopted the mantle of identity politics as their own. Only, as political commentator Laura Flanders has written, it's all identity and no politics.[5]

While true equality for people of color and women remains elusive, "diversity" is now a moral value, one so conventional that even President Bush touts it as an ideal. "I strongly support diversity of all kinds," he bragged in 2003.[6] Today phrases like "hate speech"— twisted to signal attacks on conservatives—and "color blind"—held up as the ethical alternative to affirmative action—make up the modern conservative moral vocabulary. According to Fox News, "people of faith" are being persecuted the way people of color were decades ago.[7] Thus, counterintuitively, the Republican Party, and the Bush administration specifically, have appropriated the language of the civil rights era and embraced the politics of identity, if not on the level of social policy than at least in the realm of rhetoric.

Students for Academic Freedom, David Horowitz's latest

project, plays this card perfectly. Last year I interviewed young people enlisted in his struggle to get left-leaning "tenured radicals" out of the classroom. Their efforts focus on passing an Academic Bill of Rights, a bill that would grant conservatives minority status on campuses, a move that effectively turns identity politics on its head. "If you look at the 1960s, it has impacted the conservative movement with the whole 'intellectual diversity' thing," a freshman at Brown University told me. "The conservatives have adopted the language of the radical left in the 60s–freedom, freedom of speech–and it's definitely been a powerful message. Even professors who aren't sympathetic to our movement, they've picked up on it."

From college Republicans to the Oval Office, these folks expertly play on our assumptions about identity to promote their agenda.

Democrats, in the meantime, desperately seek to shake the charge of pandering to minorities and "special interests." Still technically the party of affirmative action and women's right to choose, Democratic officials are loath to admit so publicly, deathly afraid of alienating a "moral majority" that has become increasingly antiquated with each passing election. The result has been a steady move to the political center, an embrace of a big-business agenda, and an awkward mumbling on most of the issues at the center of the culture wars.

Today those who need a scapegoat for the Democratic Party's four-decade-long foundering often point the finger at the antiwar, women's, and civil rights groups of the 60s and 70s.[8] Michael Tomasky's much-discussed May 2006 *American Prospect* cover story, "Party in Search of a Notion," does just that. Liberalism's crisis, he argues, can be traced back to this period and the "rights-based" activists "guilty of defenestrating the idea of the common good."[9] (If working to abolish sexism and racism is not a struggle of the common good, I don't know what is.)

Tomasky, it seems, is still upset about 1972, the year Senator George McGovern won the Democratic Party's presidential nomination but lost to Nixon in a landslide. In response to 1968's

violent Democratic National Convention (DNC) in Chicago–
historic for the antiwar demonstrations in the streets, the images
of police beating protesters broadcast live on television, and the
heated exchanges between delegates inside–a series of reforms
were initiated within the Democratic Party. Most importantly, the
reforms mandated quotas for proportional Black, female, and
youth representation: a state's delegations had to be as diverse as
the state itself. As a result the 1972 convention more accurately re-
flected the American populace than any before or after: the number
of African-American and female delegates tripled; representatives
under the age of 30 quadrupled. Yet McGovern's campaign, based
on his long-standing opposition to the war in Vietnam, lacked the
support of many Middle Americans, especially working-class white
men.

Today, the ghost of 1972 lingers on, even as most of the
nomination reforms have fallen to the wayside. That year's convention will forever be remembered as disastrously overrun with
Black Power advocates, women's libbers, and homosexuals–not
as the most integrated convention in history, as one that defiantly
opposed the killing in Vietnam, or as the convening of a presidential campaign victimized by the "dirty tricks" now known as
Watergate. Today it's easier for people like Tomasky to point the
finger at the practitioners of identity politics than take on the Democratic Party's bigger problems: institutional racism, classism, and
sexism; the increasing influence of corporate money on elections
and platform; the Party's cowardly stance on the war (Vietnam or
Iraq, you pick); and the Democrats' continual demoralization and
dismissal of its progressive base.

Ironically, all this is occurring as the Right embraces identity politics with aplomb.

To make this leap, the masterminds of the Bush administration
had to reconcile the fundamental disconnect between conservative
philosophy and identity politics. They did this by updating the
narrative of the self-made man, making him Latino or transform-
ing him into an Asian-American woman. Cast a spotlight on these
colorful self-improvement success stories and presto! The Repub-

lican Party becomes a beacon of diversity. Figures like Clarence Thomas, Elaine Chao, and Alberto Gonzales are portrayed not as victims looking for special treatment, but as exceptional people who, through determination and hard work, capitalized on the opportunities presented to them. Identity politics, so repurposed, celebrate individual, as opposed to shared, experience and promotes competition over community. Rice's background assures her mythical status accordingly: There is the discrimination her family faced in Birmingham, her precocity as a sixteen-year-old college student, her father's instruction that she be "twice as good" to triumph over injustice, and the fact that she did so. All of this proves her prodigious and unparalleled abilities, her meritoriousness, her specialness. And Rice's innumerable accomplishments, we are told, prove that our society rewards those who are driven, diligent, and deserving, regardless of their race, class, or sex.

This atomization is a far cry from the progressive vision in which identity provides a means to create collective power through common experience. And it's high time the Left reclaimed the language of solidarity so viciously retooled to serve the selfish ambitions of the Right instead of running away from it.

For many of us, belonging to a disadvantaged minority (whether by race, gender, sexual orientation, physical ability, or age) presents an opportunity to gain insight into larger, structural injustices in our society, which is a good thing. But Rice proves this is not always the case. Greed, hubris, and indifference to the suffering of others, sadly, appear to be equal-opportunity afflictions. So how is someone concerned about racial and sexual equality supposed to deal with a figure like Condoleezza Rice? The answer is clear: We must submit the actions of the secretary of state to critical analysis no less rigorous than our analysis of any other public official. Such is the only egalitarian approach. To show true respect for Rice as a Black woman is to judge her by her words and deeds, not her shoes or her illusory romantic liaisons. By deconstructing the mystique in which she's shrouded, we'll see, no matter how compelling or exceptional she may be, that Rice is not that different than the good old boys she hangs with, and that real diversity remains an honorable, if elusive, ideal.

Notes

1. http://www.whitehouse.gov/nsc/nss/2006/nss2006.pdf and http://www.state.gov/secretary/rm/2006/59306.htm; also see Pat M. Holt, "The risks of proactive US diplomacy," *Christian Science Monitor*, March 2, 2006.

2. Julian Borger, Ewen MacAskill and Jonathan Watts, "New diplomatic priorities offer snapshot of changing world order," *Guardian*, March 4, 2006.

3. Cooper, Helen, "Dance of Diplomacy Is Grist for the Gossip Mill," *New York Times*, September 13, 2006.

4. John Machacek, "Poll shows Clinton admired as leader, but divisive," *USA Today*, August 8, 2005 and http://www.pollingreport.com/2008.htm. Laura Bush's sky high approval ratings, despite her husband's sinking ones, is another example of this phenomenon. http://www.usatoday.com/news/washington/2006-05-21-laura-bush_x.htm.

5. Laura Flanders, *Bushwomen: Tales of a Cynical Species*, Verso, 2004.

6. http://www.whitehouse.gov/news/releases/2003/01/20030115-7.html.

7. Geoffrey Nunberg, *Talking Right: How Conservatives Turned Liberalism into a Tax-Raising, Latte-Drinking, Sushi-Eating, Volvo-Driving, New York Times-Reading, Body-Piercing, Hollywood-Loving, Left-Wing Freak Show*, New York: Public Affairs, 2006.

8. See Leonard Steinhorn's "Scrooge's Nightmare," *Salon*, November 24, 2005, and a survey by The New Politics Institute in 2006 which supports Steinhorn's claim, showing an increasingly Democratic, liberal/progressive orientation among young people.

9. Michael Tomasky, "Party In Search of a Notion," *American Prospect*, May 2006.

SOMEBODY BLEW UP AMERICA

Amiri Baraka

(All thinking people
oppose terrorism
both domestic
& international...
But one should not
be used
To cover the other)

They say it's some terrorist, some
   barbaric
         A Rab, in
 Afghanistan
It wasn't our American terrorists
It wasn't the Klan or the Skinheads
Or the them that blows up nigger
Churches, or reincarnates us on Death Row
It wasn't Trent Lott
Or David Duke or Giuliani
Or Schundler, Helms retiring

It wasn't
the gonorrhea in costume
the white sheet diseases
that have murdered Black people
terrorized reason and sanity
most of humanity, as they please

They say (who say?) Who do the saying
Who is them paying
Who tell the lies
Who in disguise
Who had the slaves
Who got the bux out the Bucks

Who got fat from plantations
Who genocided Indians
Tried to waste the Black nation

Who live on Wall Street
 The first plantation
Who cut your nuts off
Who rape your ma
Who lynch your pa

Who got the tar, who got the feathers
Who had the match, who set the fires
Who killed and hired
Who say they God & still be the Devil

Who the biggest only
Who the most goodest
Who do Jesus resemble

Who created everything
Who the smartest
Who the greatest

Who the richest
Who say you ugly and they the goodlookingest

Who define art
Who define science

Who made the bombs
Who made the guns

Who bought the slaves, who sold them

Who called you them names
Who say Dahmer wasn't insane

  Who / Who / Who

Who stole Puerto Rico
Who stole the Indies, the Philippines, Manhattan
 Australia & the Hebrides
Who forced opium on the Chinese

Who own them buildings
Who got the money
Who think you funny
Who locked you up
Who own the papers

Who owned the slave ship
Who run the army

Who thc fake president
Who the ruler
Who the banker

  Who / Who / Who

Who own the mine
Who twist your mind
Who got bread
Who need peace
Who you think need war

Who own the oil
Who do no toil
Who own the soil
Who is not a nigger
Who is so great ain't nobody bigger

Who own this city

Who own the air
Who own the water

Who own your crib
Who rob and steal and cheat and murder
  and make lies the truth
Who call you uncouth

Who live in the biggest house
Who do the biggest crime
Who go on vacation anytime

Who killed the most niggers
Who killed the most Jews
Who killed the most Italians
Who killed the most Irish
Who killed the most Africans
Who killed the most Japanese
Who killed the most Latinos

    Who / Who / Who

Who own the ocean

Who own the airplanes
Who own the malls
Who own television
Who own radio

Who own what ain't even known to be owned
Who own the owners that ain't the real owners

Who own the suburbs
Who suck the cities
Who make the laws

Who made Bush president
Who believe the confederate flag need to be flying
Who talk about democracy and be lying
 WHO / WHO / WHO

Who the Beast in Revelations
Who 666
Who decide
 Jesus get crucified

Who the Devil on the real side
Who got rich from Armenian genocide

Who the biggest terrorist
Who change the bible
Who killed the most people
Who do the most evil
Who don't worry about survival

Who have the colonies
Who stole the most land
Who rule the world

Who say they good but only do evil
Who the biggest executioner

  Who / Who / Who

Who own the oil
Who want more oil
Who told you what you think that later
  you find out a lie
  Who / Who / ???

Who found bin Laden, maybe they Satan
Who pay the CIA
Who knew the bomb was gonna blow
Who know why the terrorists
 Learned to fly in Florida, San Diego

Who know why five Israelis was filming the explosion
 And cracking they sides at the notion

Who need fossil fuel when the sun ain't goin' nowhere

Who make the credit cards
Who get the biggest tax cut
Who walked out of the Conference
 Against Racism
Who killed Malcolm, Kennedy & his Brother
Who killed Dr. King
Who would want to do such a thing?
 Are they linked to the murder of Lincoln?

Who invaded Grenada
Who made money from apartheid
Who keep the Irish a colony
Who overthrow Chile and Nicaragua later

Who killed David Sibeko, Chris Hani,
  The same ones who killed Biko, Cabral,
        Allende, Che Guevara, Sandino

Who killed Kabila, the ones who wasted Lumumba,
  Mondlane, Betty Shabazz, Princess Margaret, Ralph
  Featherstone, Little Bobby

Who locked up Mandela, Dhoruba, Geronimo,
Assata, Mumia, Garvey, Dashiell Hammett, Alphaeus
  Hutton

Who killed Huey Newton, Fred Hampton,
  Medgar Evers, Mikey Smith, Walter Rodney
Was it the ones who tried to poison Fidel
Who tried to keep the Vietnamese oppressed

Who put a price on Lenin's head

Who put the Jews in ovens,
  And who helped them do it
Who said "America First"
  And ok'd the yellow stars
        Who / Who / ^^

Who killed Rosa Luxembourg, Liebknecht
Who murdered the Rosenbergs
  And all the good people iced,
  tortured, assassinated, vanished

Who got rich from Algeria, Libya, Haiti,
  Iran, Iraq, Saudi, Kuwait, Lebanon,
  Syria, Egypt, Jordan, Palestine

Who cut off people's hands in the Congo
Who invented AIDS Who put germs

in the Indians blankets
Who thought up "The Trail of Tears"

Who blew up the Maine
& started the Spanish American War
Who got Sharon back in power
Who backed Batista, Hitler, Bilbo,
   Chiang Kai-shek
            Who WHO WHO

Who decided Affirmative Action had to go
  Reconstruction, The New Deal, the New
  Frontier, The Great Society

Who do Tom Ass Clarence work for
Who doo doo come out the Colon's mouth
Who know what kind of Skeeza is a Condoleezza
Who pay Connelly to be a wooden negro
Who give Genius Awards to Homo Locus
  Subsidere

Who overthrew Nkrumah, Bishop,
Who poison Robeson,
  Who try to put DuBois in jail
Who frame Rap Jamil al Amin, who frame
  the Rosenbergs, Garvey, The Scottsboro Boys,
  The Hollywood Ten

Who set the Reichstag Fire

Who knew the World Trade Center was gonna get
  bombed
Who told 4,000 Israeli workers at the Twin Towers
  To stay home that day
Why did Sharon stay away?

Who, Who, Who
 Explosion of Owl the newspaper say
The devil face cd be seen Who WHO who WHO

Who make money from war
Who make dough from fear and lies
Who want the world like it is
Who want the world to be ruled by imperialism and
national oppression and terror violence, and hunger
and poverty.

Who is the ruler of Hell?
Who is the most powerful?

Who you know ever
Seen God?

But everybody seen
The Devil

Like an Owl exploding
In your life in your brain in your self
Like an Owl who know the devil
All night, all day if you listen, Like an Owl
Exploding in fire. We hear the questions rise
In terrible flame like the whistle of a crazy dog

Like the acid vomit of the fire of Hell
Who and Who and WHO (+) who who ^
Whoooo and Whoooooooooooooooooooooooooooo!

now it can be told!

dr. condoleezza rice

[herself]

worldwide sleep-in girl extraordinaire in crisis!

a page drama

hattie gossett

backstage at the dr. rice page drama

where are we?
cyberspace.

what time is it?
nation time. spring 2006.

who are these people?
enchilada caliente: usa justice department spymaster.
iced rummy: usa defense department spymaster.
dirty rice cakes: usa secretary of state dr. condoleezza rice.
sleep-in: person who does domestic work & lives at the home[s] of
the employer.
worldwide sleep-in girls & boys foundation [wwsig&bf]: nonprofit
nonpartisan foundation advocating for the rites of sleep-ins.
furry taco cumcum grls: sex workers.
bushie boy: usa president george w. bush.
old daddy bush & grannie barb: parents of bushie boy.
shotgun: usa vice president dick cheney.

what is going on?
mr. caliente & his spies pick up on wwsig&bf & their very sensitive
e-report about dr. rice. is wwsig&bf really an enclave of terrorists?
right away mr. caliente e-mails the report to mr. rummy suggest-
ing that maybe they can use wwsig&bf to carry out their own plot
against dr. rice. mr. caliente loves referring to government notables
by their secret service code names. he uses the word emission to
mean email transmission. will dr. rice take a death hit simply cuz
the guys on her own team did nothing to prevent it? the emission
from mr. caliente to mr. rummy is interrupted a couple times. is
there a subtext to the relationship between mr. rummy & mr. caliente? how many people in your extended family started out as/still
are sleep-ins?

lights up at the dr. rice page drama

from: *enchilada caliente*
            torture?whynot?@justice.gov
to: *iced rummy*
            bombtheevildoers!now!@defense.gov
subject: *no more dirty rice cakes?!! emission #1*
date: *06/06/06 @ 06:06:06 p.m.*

its me your enchilada guy here at justice. thought you & your crew at defense should see this scorching document my internet spy guys just uncovered. betcha never heard of these nutcases—"worldwide sleep-in girls & boys foundation"? oxymorons anyone? now dont go confusing them with our furry taco cumcum grls you long tall cool thing you ha! ha! its not that kind of sleep-in. ha! ha! our analysts say these nutcases are a terrorist cell fronting as domestics. am sending their scorcher along as an attachment to this note. maybe we arent the only ones who are sick of dirty rice cakes? huh? stay tuned.

from: special commission/world wide sleep-in girls & boys foundation [wwsig&bf]
          gettingpaid@goodhelp.org
to: wwsig&bf full membership
subject: final update on: [1] changing our name [2] dr. rice & project disappear
date: 5/01/06 @ 5:01:06 a.m

whats up? this final update—which also goes out via fax & audio cassette—summarizes months of wwsig&bf regional roundtables concerning: [1] changing our name [2] activating project disappear on dr. condoleezza rice. it also calls for a vote on these 2 critical matters. your ballot is at the end of this update.

#1. whats in a name? wwsig&bf is a nonpartisan nonprofit foundation whose sole mission is the wellbeing of its members who until now were known as sleep-in girls & boys or just sleep-ins. ranging in age from 7 or 8 to 70 or 80 wwsig&bf members are of all genders & races & render interminable hours of domestic service in & around the home[s] of their employers—big daddy & ms anne a/k/a massa & missie—& reside there too as opposed to day workers who return to their own homes at the end of each day. by no means is big daddy always white rich or hetero.

those who underestimate us still insist on equating sleep-ins with traitorous toms & mumbling mammys & disease-ridden lite-fingered sex workers—historical blindness of the highest order. [should we re-publish our underground classic "ground glass in the biscuits & other secret big-house recipes"? after all every houseslave wasnt a sellout & every fieldhand wasnt a revolutionary. things were/are way more complicated than that.] besides our profession predates the american empire by eons. whats new is that we came together from around the world to create wwsig&bf to advocate for our interests.

today many younger wwsig&bf members [under 40] say that going forward into the 21st century we should change our name from sleep-in girls & boys to something like live-in domestic service providers or residential household staff. they say sleep-in girls & boys is an american name for a universal & timeless profession. in other times & countries we were/are known by other names. its also a nasty & undignified ahistorical reflection of age & gender disrespect. many older members say sleep-in girls & boys is mostly what our 19th & 20th century forebears were called & it is how we are referred to in the history books & so we should hold to this designation out of respect & a certain ironic historical sense. please have your say on the ballot.

#2. moving rite along: dr. rice & project disappear. in the 1970s days of usa world glory president richard m nixon thrilled over his green power trumps black power domestic insurgency victory thanks to dirtytricks perpetrated by the cointelpro spy network. despite the humiliation of vietnam he positively glowed over the success of his economic incursions into china. big daddy nixon reigned supreme—til watergate anyway. at his rite hand he had dr. henry "ironhand" kissinger as his secretary of state. dr. ironhand shaped & influenced power. nothing—not even an ivory toothpick on the banquet table of state—moved without his say so.

today in 2006 president george w. bush rages round the planet in search of victory over the evil doers. flashing the pox americana freedom flag rag he bullies sovereign nations —gimme that oil! my god is supreme!—then he pouts & clutches his moneybags & sends war machines when things dont turn out like he paid for them to. as secretary of state he has his daddygirl woman dr. condoleezza "up by her bootstraps" rice. sadly dr. rice isnt at the rite hand of power. she doesnt shape or influence power. rather she runs briskly along cleaning up behind power. she runs briskly along cleaning up behind big daddy w & his boys & making everything they do look rite as raindrops on roses & whiskers on catfish. she actually lives on the texas plantation of big daddy w & ms. laura & family. she is so devoted. she is always working. even when she is off from work she is still working cuz she has no home of her own. though she acts like she doesnt know it dr. rice is in fact the worlds most high profile sleep-in girl. dr. sleep-in.

our regional roundtables indicated that it is exceedingly disturbing to nearly all wwsig&bf members that dr. sleep-in acts like she doesnt know a 21st century sleep-in girl is entitled to paid days off & wages sufficient to maintain a home away from big daddy. of course poor dr. sleep-in cant see herself as a profoundly abused homeless sleepwalking sleep-in daddygirl in need of help. more to the point for us: not only does dr. sleep-in need help for her own sake—she needs help *for our sake*. project disappear will do the job.

so many wwsig&bf members think project disappear involves exerting physical violence against dr. sleep-in. please. we dont intend to hurt a hair on the head of dr. sleep-in. project disappear involves rescue & rehab & rebirth. she would be rescued from big daddy. she would be rehabilitated from her daddygirl meds & mindset. finally she would be reborn as a new & harmless someone in a better place far far away. project disappear is the best thing for her & us. with her worldwide visibility she is too dangerous. besides, if we dont take care of her who will?

subject: no more dirty rice cakes?!! emission #2
hows that grabbing you? huh? its me enchilada again. i put the nutcase terrorists
on pause for a minute. we now have 24/7 coverage on them. in fact i have actu-
ally set up a tiny colony in their system. i am coming to you via a direct feed from
their computer files. ha! ha! should their emission be sent to bushie boy with yet
another warning of the dangers inherent in his policy of continually promoting
dirty rice cakes over deserving ivy leaf bluegum i mean blueblood whiteboys? why
does he keep ignoring us about this? this condi 4 prez thing isnt a joke anymore.
we could be stuck with this smartmouthed biglipped arrogant darky in designer
suits & pumps as president! ay that hair! is bushie boy darkmeat pussywhipped
or what? ay dios! everyone is sick of her but no one has the balls to move. i say
why be a master of the universe if you dont use the power? i say ice her! you &
me we have talked about this forever. its time to move. i say one supersized order
of eternal hourly rotations of thorough thrashings & forced feedings in the lost
dungeon coming up. equal opportunity sucks! huh? o.k. back to the nutcase terror-
ists. stay tuned.

subject: final update on: [1] changing our name; [2] dr. rice & project disappear.

#2a. the heart of the matter: stand up 4 r rites & boundaries.

as most wwsig&b members know we have standards & rites & boundaries which we do our best to tease big daddy & missie into respecting. our best tickle stick is the promise of days of absence. [we all know how big daddy & missie fear being alone.] our minimum standard package includes wages sufficient to maintain a home of ones own away from big daddy—even if that home is only a furnished room. it also designates every thursday & every other sunday & the last 2 weeks in august [or the local equivalent] as paid days off. this is our bottom line—for which blood continues to be spilled.

dr. sleep-in ignores all rites & boundaries. she thinks big daddy w is her best friend. shes especially close to old daddy bush & grannie barb. she was so happy when they passed her along from their service across generational lines to the service of their boy george—just like massa & missie always pass on truly trusty sleep-ins to their young uns who are carving out a new piece of the power. dr. sleep-in was a standout among passed along staffers like bushbrain rove & cheney & rumsfeld & powell et al. & thats how she entered the inner circle.

the problem is that all the et al. guys go home but dr. sleep-in doesnt cuz she is homeless. they may not have much energy for anything & may need ever more fierce meds to help them unwind on their home away from the beltway photo op weekends [stipulated in their employment contracts] & ever more & more fierce meds to rewind them back up when its time [finally] to get back to work. but they do go home. each has an away from the beltway home complete with spouse & kiddies & sometimes a pet or 2. each lives [officially anyway] in this home with spouse & kiddies & a pet or 2 though they are mostly in their beltway apartments or hotel rooms with their beltway bed buddies. on weekends they are out in the bushes on catered fishing & hunting jaunts. some of us serve drinks & change the sheets at those locations. the thing is this: why was her new york times chamber music photo op shot in her beltway apartment? she has a rite to her own away from the beltway home just like the et al. guys. as for spouse or kiddies or pet thats up to her.

even with her raging daddygirl hormones how could dr. sleep-in not know such an essential factor as her rites & boundaries? with all her advanced education she still needs to learn to step up & stand up. some members wonder if she is even getting paid. who knows? what we know is that when you are with big daddy all the time & you think he is your best friend you dont even have to carry money cuz everything is just…taken care of. then one day you wake up &….

we cant afford for dr. sleep-in to wake up like that. with her worldwide visibility & her continual state of denial she is making it bad for the rest of us. how can we **SERVER CONNECTION? ERROR. STOP. STOP.**

subject: no more dirty rice cakes?!! emission #3

SERVER CONNECTION? ERROR. STOP. STOP.

!huh? damned machines acting up again. shit fuck diablo! cut off in the middle of the oh here it comes back again. stay tuned.

subject: final update on: [1] changing our name; [2] dr. rice & project disappear.
keep holding big daddys feet to the fire when there she is on tv every day denying even the need to think about rites & boundaries—let alone have any?

we cant let our position weaken any further. big daddy is already getting way too much wiggle room about our paid weekly time off. depending on how cheap he is our every thursday off could start rite after dinner on wednesday evening or not until after breakfast on thursday morning. that day off could end at 11 p.m. sharp on thursday nite or we could be allowed to spend the nite at home & report back to massa in time for work on friday morning. his whim determines whether our paid every other sunday off starts rite after dinner on saturday evening or not til after breakfast on sunday morning & whether we can stay home til monday morning. we must hold the line.

#2b. we are on our own side. wwsig&bf members arent the only people who have a real problem with dr. sleep-in. she is viciously hated by so many for so many reasons. some people are just pain jealous. others—not all of them white—hate her cuz she is a person of color. others—not all of them men—hate her cuz she is a woman. so many hate her just cuz of her hair. its amazing. many who still deliver their partisan allegiance on demand to the democrats year after year reallyreally hate her. of course these dems would probably love everything about her they now find so abhorrent if only she cleaned up behind them like she does for republicans. after all you gotta love her fierceness as she circles the globe in her private jet telling the biggest bodacious boldface lies out of her cute little gaptoothed mouth unwaveringly rite into the camera in her persistent & determined daddygirl sunday school squeaky clean voice & her demure pearl earrings.

during our roundtable travels we commissioners actually met secretly with some people from the draft condi in 2008 democrat splinter group. yes. a minority of a minority of a minority. they like to imagine that if dr. sleep-in had been working for president bill clinton she surely wouldnt have pretended to ignore what was going on with him & miss monica like his staffers did. look where that "the personal isnt political wink wink" stuff got them. the condi dems swear she would have slapped a lock on massa billy boys zipper & swept miss monica & her betrayer out the side door so fast—after first paying them off—your ears would have popped.

these condi dems swear that when charming massa billy was preparing to sign something stupid like n.a.f.t.a. to send so many jobs overseas or welfare reform to increase the homeless population she would have stomped so hard on his bunions in her black leather spike heeled boots til he peed all over himself & screamed for mercy & threw that mess in the trash where it belonged.

yeah. what have they been smoking? we stand apart from dems who hate dr. sleep-in simply cuz she isnt flying & lying for the daddies on their side of the aisle. thats too easy. as a nonpartisan foundation we arent on either side of the aisle. how can we be when one side takes us for granted while the other side just takes us? we are our own side.

#2c. our good thing is good to the world. dr. sleep-in is tripping which is causing raw sewage to threaten our parade. we cant let her make us blow our good thing. insufficient & unsteady as it is our good thing builds schools homes hospitals & houses of worship great & small. it buys home entertainment centers knockoff designer jeans cellphones & electrical generators & bounces rite back as worldwide taxes & profits. whole communities & nations depend on us. imagine what we could do with a real living wage & equitable profit sharing? but big daddy says he cant pay us what we are worth cuz he has to pump cash into the trickle down effect though no one we know has ever benefited from this effect.

our detractors say we neglect our kids in favor of big daddy & his kids. but what about the corporate hotshots who dont have time for their kids cuz they are always taking care of big daddys bidness? what about how so many of those hotshots sleep on the office couch nite after nite—so scared to miss a minute? are they the new sleep-ins in denial or what? what about when their kids are confined to military style rehabs cuz they are out of control? are their kids better off with corporate neglectful wage slave parents rather than sleep-in wage-slaves? isnt the main thing here that we are all still wage slaves too scared to take even half a day off from big daddys bidness for our families/ourselves?

today is may 1. as usual our office is closed for may day. this year we are also closed for "the day without immigrants." we worked all nite finalizing this report so it can go out before the start of the business day. now we are on our way to breakfast & then to the rally. "yes we can!"

well that does it. everything is up to you wwsig&bf members now. should we carry out project disappear on dr. rice? please have your say on the ballot.

#3. the ballot. please complete this ballot & send it back immediately. be sure to answer each question.
[1] shall we change our name? circle one: yes. no. don't care.
[2] if you answered yes to #1 check one of the following as our new name:
__worldwide sleep-in domestics foundation
__live-in private service providers worldwide foundation
__foundation for residential household staff worldwide
__live-in domestic service providers international foundation
[3] hate all the above? please write in your idea: _____
_____
[4] shall we carry out project disappear—nonviolent rescue & rehab & rebirth—on dr. rice asap? circle one: yes. no. don't care.
[5] should someone from our car & driver division disguised as her usual car & driver pick her up at an airport & whisk her away? circle one: yes. no. don't care.
[6] should she wake up from rebirth as the [select one of the following]:
__newly appointed n.f.l. commissioner a retired wealthy bachelor

nerd guy who loves to play piano sonatas read russian literature &
pamper his organic garden.

__polygamous 2nd wife of brother blingman the knockoff video
entrepreneur who will bring her to heel & dress her in baby phat
& have her switching in the kitchen whipping up tofu porkchops &
beanpies & lay a solid humping on her every other nite so she can
pop at least one baby per year.

__eunuch completely devoted to training pleasure givers at our
plus size divas pleasure palace featuring food! shopping! shows!
spa! safe sex! sleeping late!

__who cares about this rehab/rebirth stuff? just return her as is to
her home planet.

[7] bonus question: should we help sweep big daddy w out the
door by endorsing "impeach the m.f. already!"

circle one: yes. no. don't care.

[8] bonus question: what shall we **SERVER CONNECTION
HAS FAILED. FAILED. SOCKET ERROR #109XY623.
ANTI-SNOOP FIREWALL. STOP.**

subject: no more dirty rice cakes?!! emission #4

**SERVER CONNECTION HAS FAILED. FAILED.
SOCKET ERROR #109XY623. ANTI-SNOOP FIREWALL.
STOP.** *what? is our site invaded?* **SERVER CONNECTION HAS
FAILED.** *emission canceled? e-address blocked? what? we lost the nutcase ter-
rorists emission? am i getting through to you? don't worry my guys will fix this.*

*anyway maybe we should just let these nutcase terrorists take care of
dirty rice cakes for us? by the way do i cc: shotgun on this? you know he isnt a
lovely camper when he thinks we have ignored him. please advice. faithfully—
your enchilada p.s. got a nu cumcum girl who cant wait to smoke 2 manly cigars
together in her furry taco! wanna play some more? still tingling from last month!
talk about sleeping in! huh? stay tuned.*

instructions for survival
1. Beat him at his own game.
2. Don't let your peers stand in your way
3. never trust anyone, especially not yourself
4. You're as good as your word, and your word
    is no good
5. Your allies are your enemies
6. vice-versa
7. fake your convictions
8. quietly kill dissent
9. keep a game face
10. occasionally wear lipstick to reveal your
    true beauty

Instructions for Survival, Kara Walker

CONTRIBUTOR NOTES

Amiri Baraka, celebrated playwright and poet, is the author of many books including *The Autobiography of Leroi Jones* and, most recently, *Tales of the Out & the Gone.*

Kate Bornstein is the author of *Hello Cruel World: 101 Alternatives to Suicide for Teens, Freaks & Other Outlaws*; *Gender Outlaw: On Men, Women and the Rest of Us*; *My Gender Notebook: How to Become a Real Man, a Real Woman, the Real You, or Something Else*; and co-author of *Nearly Roadkill: An Infobahn Erotic Thriller*, with Caitlin Sullivan. She lives in New York City.

Ann E. Butler is currently Senior Archivist at the Fales Library and Special Collections at New York University. Her interests include the documentation of contemporary performance-related and installation-based works, the preservation of analog and digital media formats, and the increasing convergence of archive and museum collection management practices for contemporary materials.

Sue Coe, activist artist and author of many books, has had a recent exhibition of her drawings at the National Museum of Women in the Arts in Washington, DC. She is the author of *How to Commit Suicide in South Africa*, among many books.

Wanda Coleman, a Guggenheim fellow, Emmy-winning script-writer, and former columnist for *Los Angeles Times* magazine, is the author of *Bathwater Wine, Mambo Hips & Make Believe, Mercuro-chrome: New Poems,* and *The Riot Inside Me: More Trials & Tremors.*

Coco Fusco is a New York-based interdisciplinary artist and writer. She has performed, lectured, exhibited and curated around the world since 1988. Fusco's performances and videos have been included in such events as The Whitney Biennial, Sydney Biennale, The Johannesburg Biennial, The Kwangju Biennale, The Shanghai Biennale, InSite 05, Transmediale, The London International Theatre Festival, VideoBrasil and Performa05. A recipient of a 2003 Herb Alpert Award in the Arts, she is an associate professor at Columbia University.

hattie gossett, a writer and performer, is the author of *presenting sister noblues* and *the pussy & cash suite.* She is a co-founding editor of *Essence Magazine* and Kitchen Table: Women of Color Press, and lives at the NYC intersection where the Republic of Harlem meets the Dominican Republic.

Rachel Holmes is a writer, broadcaster, columnist, and reviewer. From 1991 to 1998, she held professorships at the University of London and the University of Sussex. Her first book, *Scanty Particulars: The Scandalous Life and Astonishing Secret of James Barry, Queen Victoria's Most Eminent Military Doctor* (2002), was followed recently by *African Queen: The Real Life of The Hottentot Venus,* published in 2007 to coincide with the 200th anniversary of the abolition of the British slave trade. She is currently writing a life of Eleanor Marx.

Gary Indiana is the author of six novels, two books of short stories, and four books of nonfiction. He is also a noted photographer and the director of two feature films, *Pariah* and *Soap*, both to be released in 2007. He is the screenwriter of the forthcoming Mike Hodges film *The Impasse*, starring Malcolm McDowell, and is currently writing a book on Andy Warhol, to be published simultaneously with his second volume of collected essays.

Jason Mecier is currently working on a project called Celebrity Junkdrawer, in which he is creating 3-dimensional portraits of his favorite celebrities made out of their "stuff." Phyllis Diller, Morgan Fairchild, Parker Posey, Barbi Benton, Elvira, Tura Satana, Susan Tyrrell, Kathy Najimy, Bruce Vilanche, Kate Pierson, Sara Gilbert, Joan Van Ark, Dayna Devon, Heidi Fleiss and others are participating. He lives and works in San Francisco.

Jill Nelson is a writer and activist. She is the author of five books, including the best-selling memoir, *Volunteer Slavery: My Authentic Negro Experience*; the satirical novel, *Sexual Healing*. Her second novel, *Let's Get It On*, will be published in 2007. She is currently working on a polemic, *When White Men Get Scared: Imagining Democracy*. She writes a twice monthly column for NiaOnline.com.

Faith Ringgold, painter and writer, is professor emeritus at the University of California, San Diego. The recipient of more than 75 awards including 18 Honorary Doctor of Fine Arts Degrees, the National Endowment For the Arts Award for sculpture and painting, and the John Simon Guggenheim Memorial Foundation Fellowship for painting, she has written and illustrated fourteen children's books including *Tar Beach*, a modern classic for children of all ages. Ringgold's art is included in many private and public art collections including The Metropolitan Museum of Art, The National Museum of American Art, The Museum of Modern Art and The Solomon R. Guggenheim Museum.

Paul Robeson, Jr., an esteemed cultural critic, is the author of *A Black Way of Seeing: From "Liberty" to Freedom, Paul Robeson, Jr. Speaks to America: The Politics of Multiculturalism,* and *The Undiscovered Paul Robeson: An Artist's Journey.* Son of the legendary Paul Robeson, he served for more than twenty years as his father's close aide and personal representative.

Sapphire is the author of two books of poetry, *American Dreams* and *Black Wings & Blind Angels* and the award winning novel, *Push.* She lives and works in New York City.

Astra Taylor is a documentary filmmaker and writer. Her work has appeared in *Salon, Monthly Review, The Nation,* and Alternet. She is currently finishing her first book, about the contradictory legacy of the 1960s for people who have come of age in the decade's shadow.

Kara Walker, MacArthur fellow and widely acclaimed visual artist, has recently had an exhibition at the Metropolitan Museum of Art, New York. The first full-scale American museum survey of her work, "Kara Walker: My Complement, My Enemy, My Oppressor, My Love," premiered at the Walker Art Center, and will travel to the Whitney Museum of American Art, and the UCLA Hammer Museum. She lives in New York City.

Haifa Zangana was born in Baghdad in 1950. She has published three novels and three collections of short stories. She is Chair of Iraqi Committee for National Media and Culture (ICNMC), a founding member of International Association of Contemporary Iraqi Studies (IACIS), writes commentary for *The Guardian, Red Pepper,* and *Al Ahram,* and is a columnist for *Al Quds* newspaper.

ACKNOWLEDGMENTS

In late Spring 2005 my conversations with Karen Finley about the phenomenon of Condoleezza Rice inspired me to put together this book. I thank her for this and all the other ways she has enlightened me.

One of the first writers to respond to my call for contributions, hattie gossett, in all her wisdom and good humor, insisted on referring to our subject as Dr. Rice, correcting all that the informality and trivializing of "Condi" suggests.

Many thanks to my associate editors, Gavin Browning and Crystal Yakacki, for their excellent readings. And to Rex Ray, for his beautiful design.

Finally, my thanks to the contributors to this volume. Condoleezza Rice turned out to be a very difficult figure to make work about. As vexing as she is powerful, it was essential to me that she be taken seriously, even and especially as she is critiqued. I am grateful for the full and unexpected range of responses I received, and hope that the intelligence, rigor and generosity of these contributions offer an antidote of sorts to the cruelty of these times.

—AS